OpenCV By Example

Enhance your understanding of Computer Vision and image processing by developing real-world projects in OpenCV 3

Prateek Joshi

David Millán Escrivá

Vinícius Godoy

PUBLISHING

BIRMINGHAM - MUMBAI

OpenCV By Example

Copyright © 2016 Packt Publishing

First published: January 2016

Production reference: 1150116

Published by Packt Publishing Ltd.
Livery Place
35 Livery Street
Birmingham B3 2PB, UK.

ISBN 978-1-78528-094-8

www.packtpub.com

Credits

Authors
Prateek Joshi
David Millán Escrivá
Vinícius Godoy

Reviewers
Emmanuel d'Angelo
Dr. Bryan Wai-ching CHUNG
Nikolaus Gradwohl
Luis Díaz Más

Commissioning Editor
Ashwin Nair

Acquisition Editor
Tushar Gupta

Content Development Editor
Amey Varangaonkar

Technical Editor
Naveenkumar Jain

Copy Editor
Rashmi Sawant

Project Coordinator
Suzanne Coutinho

Proofreader
Safis Editing

Indexer
Hemangini Bari

Graphics
Kirk D'Penha

Production Coordinator
Shantanu N. Zagade

Cover Work
Shantanu N. Zagade

About the Authors

Prateek Joshi is a Computer Vision researcher and published author. He has over eight years of experience in this field with a primary focus on content-based analysis and deep learning. His work in this field has resulted in multiple patents, tech demos, and research papers at major IEEE conferences. He is the author of *OpenCV with Python By Example, Packt Publishing*.

He has won many hackathons using a wide variety of technologies related to image recognition. His blog has been visited by users in more than 200 countries, and he has been featured as a guest author in prominent tech magazines. He enjoys blogging on topics, such as artificial intelligence, abstract mathematics, and cryptography. You can visit his blog at www.prateekvjoshi.com.

He is an avid coder who is passionate about building game-changing products. He is particularly interested in intelligent algorithms that can automatically understand the content to produce scene descriptions in terms of constituent objects. He graduated from the University of Southern California and has worked for such companies as Nvidia, Microsoft Research, Qualcomm, and a couple of early stage start-ups in Silicon Valley. You can learn more about him on his personal website at www.prateekj.com.

I would like to thank the reviewers for helping me refine this book. I would also like to thank Packt Publishing for publishing this book. Finally, I would like to thank my family for supporting me through everything.

David Millán Escrivá was eight years old when he wrote his first program on an 8086 PC with BASIC language, which enabled the 2D plotting of BASIC equations. He started with his computer development relationship and created many applications and games.

In 2005, he completed his studies in IT from the Universitat Politécnica de Valencia with honors in human-computer interaction supported by Computer Vision with OpenCV (v0.96). He had a final project based on this subject and published it on HCI Spanish Congress.

In 2014, he completed his Master's degree in artificial intelligence, computer graphics, and pattern recognition, focusing on pattern recognition and Computer Vision.

He participated in Blender source code, an open source and 3D-software project, and worked in his first commercial movie, *Plumiferos — Aventuras voladoras*, as a computer graphics software developer.

David now has more than 13 years of experience in IT, with more than nine years of experience in Computer Vision, computer graphics, and pattern recognition, working on different projects and start-ups, applying his knowledge of Computer Vision, optical character recognition, and augmented reality.

He is the author of the *DamilesBlog* (http://blog.damiles.com), where he publishes research articles and tutorials on OpenCV, Computer Vision in general, and optical character recognition algorithms. He is the co-author of *Mastering OpenCV with Practical Computer Vision Projects Book* and also the reviewer of *GnuPlot Cookbook* by *Lee Phillips*, *OpenCV Computer Vision with Python* by *Joseph Howse*, *Instant Opencv Starter* by *Jayneil Dalal and Sohil Patel*, all published by *Packt Publishing*.

I would like thank to my wife, Izaskun, my daughter, Eider, and my son, Pau, for their unlimited patience and support in all moments. They have changed my life and made it awesome. Love you all.

I would like to thank the OpenCV team and community that gives us this wonderful library. I would also like to thank my co-authors and Packt Publishing for supporting me and helping me complete this book.

Vinícius Godoy is a computer graphics university professor at PUCPR. He started programming with C++ 18 years ago and ventured into the field of computer gaming and computer graphics 10 years ago. His former experience also includes working as an IT manager in document processing applications in Sinax, a company that focuses in BPM and ECM activities, building games and applications for Positivo Informática, including building an augmented reality educational game exposed at CEBIT and network libraries for Siemens Enterprise Communications (Unify).

As part of his Master's degree research, he used Kinect, OpenNI, and OpenCV to recognize Brazilian sign language gestures. He is currently working with medical imaging systems for his PhD thesis. He was also a reviewer of the *OpenNI Cookbook*, *Packt Publishing*.

He is also a game development fan, having a popular site entirely dedicated to the field called *Ponto V* (http://www.pontov.com.br). He is the cofounder of a start-up company called Blackmuppet. His fields of interest includes image processing, Computer Vision, design patterns, and multithreaded applications.

I would like to thank my wife, who supported me while writing this book. Her incentive and cooperation was decisive.

I would also like to thank Fabio Binder, a teacher who introduced me to computer graphics and gaming fields, which greatly helped me in my computer programming career and brought me to PUCPR, where I had access to several computer graphics-related software.

About the Reviewers

Emmanuel d'Angelo is a photography enthusiast, who managed to make his way in the image processing field. After several years of working as a consultant on various image-related high-tech projects, he is now working as a developer in a photogrammetry start-up. You can find image-related thoughts and code on his technical blog at http://www.computersdontsee.net.

Dr. Bryan, Wai-ching CHUNG is an interactive media artist and design consultant who lives in Hong Kong. His artworks have been exhibited at the World Wide Video Festival, Multimedia Art Asia Pacific, Stuttgart Film Winter Festival, Microwave International New Media Arts Festival, and the China Media Art Festival. In the former Shanghai Expo 2010, he provided interactive design consultancy to various industry leaders in Hong Kong and China. He studied computer science in Hong Kong, interactive multimedia in London, and fine art in Melbourne. He also develops software libraries for the popular open source programming language, Processing. He is the author of the book, *Multimedia Programming with Pure Data*. Currently, he is working as an assistant professor in the Academy of Visual Arts, Hong Kong Baptist University, where he teaches subjects on interactive arts, computer graphics, and multimedia. His website is http://www.magicandlove.com.

Nikolaus Gradwohl was born in 1976 in Vienna, Austria, and always wanted to become an inventor like Gyro Gearloose. When he got his first Atari, he figured out that being a computer programmer was the closest he could get to that dream. He wrote programs for nearly anything that can be programmed, ranging from an 8-bit microcontroller to mainframes for a living. In his free time, he likes to gain knowledge of programming languages and operating systems.

He is the author of *Processing 2: Creative Coding Hotshot, Packt Publishing*.

You can see some of his work on his blog at http://www.local-guru.net/.

Luis Díaz Más is a C++ software engineer currently working at Pix4D, where he plays the role of a software architect and develops image processing algorithms that are oriented toward photogrammetry and terrain mapping. He received his PhD in computer science from the University of Cordoba (Spain) that focuses on 3D reconstructions and action recognition. Earlier, he worked for CATEC, a research center for advanced aerospace technologies, where he developed the sensorial systems for UAS (Unmanned Aerial Systems). He has reviewed other OpenCV books published by Packt, and he is continuously looking forward to gaining more knowledge of different topics, such as modern C++ 11/14, Python, CUDA, OpenCL, and so on.

I would like to thank my parents for always supporting me and giving me the freedom to do what I like the most in this life. I would also like to thank my thesis directors, Rafa and Paco, who helped me in my scientific career and from whom I have learned a lot. Finally, a special mention to Celia, the woman who chose to share her life with this software freak and the one who continuously reminds me that there are more things in life apart from programming.

www.PacktPub.com

Support files, eBooks, discount offers, and more

For support files and downloads related to your book, please visit www.PacktPub.com.

Did you know that Packt offers eBook versions of every book published, with PDF and ePub files available? You can upgrade to the eBook version at www.PacktPub.com and as a print book customer, you are entitled to a discount on the eBook copy. Get in touch with us at service@packtpub.com for more details.

At www.PacktPub.com, you can also read a collection of free technical articles, sign up for a range of free newsletters and receive exclusive discounts and offers on Packt books and eBooks.

https://www2.packtpub.com/books/subscription/packtlib

Do you need instant solutions to your IT questions? PacktLib is Packt's online digital book library. Here, you can search, access, and read Packt's entire library of books.

Why subscribe?

- Fully searchable across every book published by Packt
- Copy and paste, print, and bookmark content
- On demand and accessible via a web browser

Free access for Packt account holders

If you have an account with Packt at www.PacktPub.com, you can use this to access PacktLib today and view 9 entirely free books. Simply use your login credentials for immediate access.

Table of Contents

Preface

OpenCV is one of the most popular libraries used to develop Computer Vision applications. It enables us to run many different Computer Vision algorithms in real time. It has been around for many years, and it has become the standard library in this field. One of the main advantages of OpenCV is that it is highly optimized and available on almost all the platforms.

This book starts off by giving a brief introduction of various fields in Computer Vision and the associated OpenCV functionalities in C++. Each chapter contains real-world examples and code samples to demonstrate the use cases. This helps you to easily grasp the topics and understand how they can be applied in real life. To sum it up, this is a practical guide on how to use OpenCV in C++ and build various applications using this library.

What this book covers

Chapter 1, *Getting Started with OpenCV*, covers installation steps on various operating systems and provides an introduction to the human visual system as well as various topics in Computer Vision.

Chapter 2, *An Introduction to the Basics of OpenCV*, discusses how to read/write images and videos in OpenCV, and also explains how to build a project using CMake.

Chapter 3, *Learning the Graphical User Interface and Basic Filtering*, covers how to build a graphical user interface and mouse event detector to build interactive applications.

Chapter 4, *Delving into Histograms and Filters*, explores histograms and filters and also shows how we can cartoonize an image.

Chapter 5, *Automated Optical Inspection, Object Segmentation, and Detection*, describes various image preprocessing techniques, such as noise removal, thresholding, and contour analysis.

Chapter 6, Learning Object Classification, deals with object recognition and machine learning, and how to use Support Vector Machines to build an object classification system.

Chapter 7, Detecting Face Parts and Overlaying Masks, discusses face detection and Haar Cascades, and then explains how these methods can be used to detect various parts of the human face.

Chapter 8, Video Surveillance, Background Modeling, and Morphological Operations, explores background subtraction, video surveillance, and morphological image processing and describes how they are connected to each other.

Chapter 9, Learning Object Tracking, covers how to track objects in a live video using different techniques, such as color-based and feature-based tracking.

Chapter 10, Developing Segmentation Algorithms for Text Recognition, covers optical character recognition, text segmentation, and provides an introduction to the Tesseract OCR engine.

Chapter 11, Text Recognition with Tesseract, delves deeper into the Tesseract OCR Engine to explain how it can be used for text detection, extraction, and recognition.

What you need for this book

The examples are built using the following technologies:

- OpenCV 3.0 or newer
- CMake 3.3.x or newer
- Tesseract
- Leptonica (dependency of Tesseract)
- QT (optional)
- OpenGL (optional)

Detailed installation instructions are provided in the relevant chapters.

Who this book is for

This book is for developers who are new to OpenCV and want to develop Computer Vision applications with OpenCV in C++. A basic knowledge of C++ would be helpful to understand this book. This book is also useful for people who want to get started with Computer Vision and understand the underlying concepts. They should be aware of basic mathematical concepts, such as vectors, matrices, matrix multiplication, and so on, to make the most out of this book. During the course of this book, you will learn how to build various Computer Vision applications from scratch using OpenCV.

Conventions

In this book, you will find a number of styles of text that distinguish between different kinds of information. Here are some examples of these styles, and an explanation of their meaning.

Code words in text are shown as follows: "For a basic project based on an executable build from one source code file, a two line CMakeLists.txt file is all that is needed ."

A block of code is set as follows:

```
#include "opencv2/opencv.hpp"
using namespace cv;

int main(int, char** argv)
{
  FileStorage fs2("test.yml", FileStorage::READ);
  Mat r;
  fs2["Result"] >> r;
  std::cout << r << std::endl;
  fs2.release();
  return 0;
}
```

When we wish to draw your attention to a particular part of a code block, the relevant lines or items are set in bold:

```
@Path("departments")
@Produces(MediaType.APPLICATION_JSON)
public class DepartmentResource{
//Class implementation goes here...
}
```

Any command-line input or output is written as follows:

```
C:\> setx -m OPENCV_DIR D:\OpenCV\Build\x64\vc11
```

New terms and **important words** are shown in bold. Words that you see on the screen, in menus or dialog boxes for example, appear in the text like this: "To show the control panel we can push the last tool bar button, right click in any part of **QT Window** and select **Display properties window**."

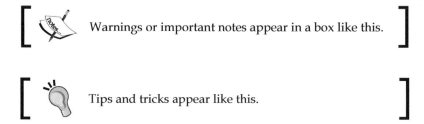

Warnings or important notes appear in a box like this.

Tips and tricks appear like this.

Reader feedback

Feedback from our readers is always welcome. Let us know what you think about this book—what you liked or may have disliked. Reader feedback is important for us to develop titles that you really get the most out of.

To send us general feedback, simply send an e-mail to feedback@packtpub.com, and mention the book title via the subject of your message.

If there is a topic that you have expertise in and you are interested in either writing or contributing to a book, see our author guide on www.packtpub.com/authors.

Customer support

Now that you are the proud owner of a Packt book, we have a number of things to help you to get the most from your purchase.

Downloading the example code

You can download the example code files for all Packt books you have purchased from your account at http://www.packtpub.com. If you purchased this book elsewhere, you can visit http://www.packtpub.com/support and register to have the files e-mailed directly to you.

Instructions for running examples are available in the README.md file present in the root folder of each project.

Downloading the color images of this book

We also provide you with a PDF file that has color images of the screenshots/diagrams used in this book. The color images will help you better understand the changes in the output. You can download this file from `https://www.packtpub.com/sites/default/files/downloads/OpenCV_By_Example_ColorImages.pdf`.

Errata

Although we have taken every care to ensure the accuracy of our content, mistakes do happen. If you find a mistake in one of our books—maybe a mistake in the text or the code—we would be grateful if you would report this to us. By doing so, you can save other readers from frustration and help us improve subsequent versions of this book. If you find any errata, please report them by visiting `http://www.packtpub.com/submit-errata`, selecting your book, clicking on the **errata submission form** link, and entering the details of your errata. Once your errata are verified, your submission will be accepted and the errata will be uploaded on our website, or added to any list of existing errata, under the Errata section of that title. Any existing errata can be viewed by selecting your title from `http://www.packtpub.com/support`.

Piracy

Piracy of copyright material on the Internet is an ongoing problem across all media. At Packt, we take the protection of our copyright and licenses very seriously. If you come across any illegal copies of our works, in any form, on the Internet, please provide us with the location address or website name immediately so that we can pursue a remedy.

Please contact us at `copyright@packtpub.com` with a link to the suspected pirated material.

We appreciate your help in protecting our authors, and our ability to bring you valuable content.

Questions

You can contact us at `questions@packtpub.com` if you are having a problem with any aspect of the book, and we will do our best to address it.

1
Getting Started with OpenCV

Computer Vision applications are interesting and useful, but the underlying algorithms are computationally intensive. With the advent of cloud computing, we are getting more processing power to work with. The OpenCV library enables you to run Computer Vision algorithms efficiently in real time. It has been around for many years and it has become the standard library in this field. One of the main advantages of OpenCV is that it is highly optimized and available on almost all platforms. The discussions in this book will cover everything, including the algorithm we are using, why we are using it, and how to implement it in OpenCV.

In this chapter, we are going to learn how to install OpenCV on various operating systems. We will discuss what OpenCV offers out of the box and the various things that we can do using the in-built functions.

By the end of this chapter, you will be able to answer the following questions:

* How do humans process visual data and how do they understand image content?

* What can we do with OpenCV and what are the various modules available in OpenCV that can be used to achieve those things?

* How to install OpenCV on Windows, Linux, and Mac OS X?

Understanding the human visual system

Before we jump into OpenCV functionalities, we need to understand why those functions were built in the first place. It's important to understand how the human visual system works so that you can develop the right algorithms. The goal of the Computer Vision algorithms is to understand the content of images and videos. Humans seem to do it effortlessly! So, how do we get machines to do it with the same accuracy?

Let's consider the following figure:

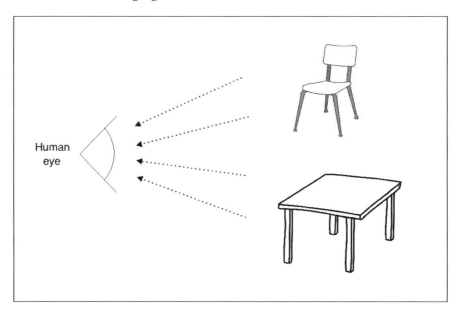

The human eye captures all the information that comes along such as color, shapes, brightness, and so on. In the preceding image, the human eye captures all the information about the two main objects and stores it in a certain way. Once we understand how our system works, we can take advantage of this to achieve what we want. For example, here are a few things we need to know:

- Our visual system is more sensitive to low frequency content than high frequency content. Low frequency content refers to planar regions where pixel values don't change rapidly and high frequency content refers to regions with corners and edges, where pixel values fluctuate a lot. You will have noticed that we can easily see if there are blotches on a planar surface, but it's difficult to spot something like that on a highly textured surface.

- The human eye is more sensitive to changes in brightness as compared to changes in color.

- Our visual system is sensitive to motion. We can quickly recognize if something is moving in our field of vision even though we are not directly looking at it.

- We tend to make a mental note of salient points in our field of vision. Let's consider a white table with four black legs and a red dot at one of the corners of the table surface. When you look at this table, you'll immediately make a mental note that the surface and legs have opposing colors and there is a red dot on one of the corners. Our brain is really smart that way! We do this automatically so that we can immediately recognize it if we encounter it again.

To get an idea of our field of view, let's take a look at the top view of a human and the angles at which we see various things:

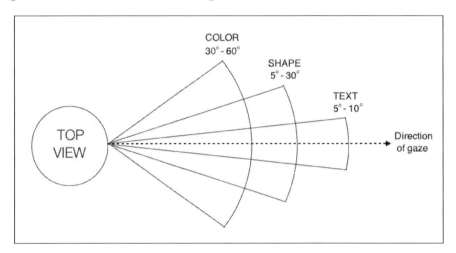

Our visual system is actually capable of a lot more things, but this should be good enough to get us started. You can explore further by reading up on Human Visual System Models on the internet.

How do humans understand image content?

If you look around, you will see a lot of objects. You may encounter many different objects every day, and you recognize them almost instantaneously without any effort. When you see a chair, you don't wait for a few minutes before realizing that it is, in fact, a chair. You just know that it's a chair right away! Now, on the other hand, computers find it very difficult to do this task. Researchers have been working for many years to find out why computers are not as good as we are at this.

To get an answer to this question, we need to understand how humans do it. The visual data processing happens in the ventral visual stream. This ventral visual stream refers to the pathway in our visual system that is associated with object recognition. It is basically a hierarchy of areas in our brain that helps us recognize objects. Humans can recognize different objects effortlessly, and we can cluster similar objects together. We can do this because we have developed some sort of invariance toward objects of the same class. When we look at an object, our brain extracts the salient points in such a way that factors such as orientation, size, perspective, and illumination don't matter.

A chair that is double the normal size and rotated by 45 degrees is still a chair. We can easily recognize it because of the way we process it. Machines cannot do this so easily. Humans tend to remember an object based on its shape and important features. Regardless of how the object is placed, we can still recognize it. In our visual system, we build these hierarchical invariances with respect to position, scale, and viewpoint that help us to be very robust.

If you look deeper in our system, you will see that humans have cells in their visual cortex that can respond to shapes, such as curves and lines. As we move further along our ventral stream, we will see more complex cells that are trained to respond to more complex objects, such as trees, gates, and so on. The neurons along our ventral stream tend to show an increase in the size of the receptive field. This is coupled with the fact that the complexity of their preferred stimuli increases as well.

Why is it difficult for machines to understand image content?

We now understand how visual data enters the human visual system and how our system processes it. The issue is that we still don't completely understand how our brain recognizes and organizes this visual data. We just extract some features from images and ask the computer to learn from them using machine learning algorithms. We still have those variations such as shape, size, perspective, angle, illumination, occlusion, and so on. For example, the same chair looks very different to a machine when you look at it from the side view. Humans can easily recognize that it's a chair regardless of how it's presented to us. So, how do we explain this to our machines?

One way to do this would be to store all the different variations of an object, including *sizes*, *angles*, *perspectives*, and so on. But this process is cumbersome and time-consuming! Also, it's actually not possible to gather data that can encompass every single variation. The machines will consume a huge amount of memory and a lot of time to build a model that can recognize these objects. Even with all this, if an object is partially occluded, computers still won't be able to recognize it. This is because they think that this is a new object. So, when we build a Computer Vision library, we need to build the underlying functional blocks that can be combined in many different ways to formulate complex algorithms. OpenCV provides a lot of these functions and they are highly optimized. So, once we understand what OpenCV provides out of the box, we can use it effectively to build interesting applications. Let's go ahead and explore this in the next section.

What can you do with OpenCV?

Using OpenCV, you can pretty much do every Computer Vision task that you can think of. Real-life problems require you to use many blocks together to achieve the desired result. So, you just need to understand what modules and functions to use to get what you want. Let's understand what OpenCV can do out of the box.

In-built data structures and input/output

One of the best things about OpenCV is that it provides a lot of in-built primitives to handle operations related to image processing and Computer Vision. If you have to write something from scratch, you will have to define things, such as an *image*, *point*, *rectangle*, and so on. These are fundamental to almost any Computer Vision algorithm. OpenCV comes with all these basic structures out of the box, and they are contained in the `core` module. Another advantage is that these structures have already been optimized for speed and memory, so you don't have to worry about the implementation details.

The `imgcodecs` module handles reading and writing image files. When you operate on an input image and create an output image, you can save it as a JPG or a PNG file with a simple command. You will be dealing with a lot of video files when you are working with cameras. The `videoio` module handles everything related to the input/output of video files. You can easily capture a video from a webcam or read a video file in many different formats. You can even save a bunch of frames as a video file by setting properties such as frames per second, frame size, and so on.

Image processing operations

When you write a Computer Vision algorithm, there are a lot of basic image processing operations that you will use over and over again. Most of these functions are present in the `imgproc` module. You can do things such as image filtering, morphological operations, geometric transformations, color conversions, drawing on images, histograms, shape analysis, motion analysis, feature detection, and so on. Let's consider the following figure:

The right-hand side image is a rotated version of the left-hand side image. We can do this transformation with a single line in OpenCV. There is another module called `ximgproc` that contains advanced image processing algorithms such as structured forests for edge detection, domain transform filters, adaptive manifold filters, and so on.

Building GUI

OpenCV provides a module called `highgui` that handles all the high-level user interface operations. Let's say that you are working on a problem and you want to check what the image looks like before you proceed to the next step. This module has functions that can be used to create windows to display images and/or video. There is also a waiting function that will wait until you hit a key on your keyboard before it goes to the next step. There is a function that can detect mouse events as well. This is very useful to develop interactive applications. Using this functionality, you can draw rectangles on these input windows and then proceed based on the selected region.

Consider the following image:

As you can see, we have drawn a green rectangle on the image and applied a *negative film* effect to that region. Once we have the coordinates of this rectangle, we can operate only on that region.

Video analysis

Video analysis includes tasks such as analyzing the motion between successive frames in a video, tracking different objects in a video, creating models for video surveillance, and so on. OpenCV provides a module called `video` that can handle all of this. There is a module called `videostab` that deals with video stabilization. Video stabilization is an important part of video cameras. When you capture videos by holding the camera in your hands, it's hard to keep your hands perfectly steady. If you look at that video as it is, it will look bad and jittery. All modern devices use video stabilization techniques to process the videos before they are presented to the end user.

3D reconstruction

3D reconstruction is an important topic in Computer Vision. Given a set of 2D images, we can reconstruct the 3D scene using the relevant algorithms. OpenCV provides algorithms that can find the relationship between various objects in these 2D images to compute their 3D positions. We have a module called `calib3d` that can handle all this. This module can also handle camera calibration, which is essential to estimate the parameters of the camera. These parameters are basically the internal parameters of any given camera that uses them to transform the captured scene into an image. We need to know these parameters to design algorithms, or else we might get unexpected results. Let's consider the following figure:

As shown in the preceding image, the same object is captured from multiple poses. Our job is to reconstruct the original object using these 2D images.

Feature extraction

As discussed earlier, the human visual system tends to extract the salient features from a given scene so that it can be retrieved later. To mimic this, people started designing various feature extractors that can extract these salient points from a given image. Some of the popular algorithms include **SIFT (Scale Invariant Feature Transform)**, **SURF (Speeded Up Robust Features)**, **FAST (Features from Accelerated Segment Test)**, and so on. There is a module called features2d that provides functions to detect and extract all these features. There is another module called xfeatures2d that provides a few more feature extractors, some of which are still in the experimental phase. You can play around with these if you get a chance. There is also a module called bioinspired that provides algorithms for biologically inspired Computer Vision models.

Object detection

Object detection refers to detecting the location of an object in a given image. This process is not concerned with the type of object. If you design a chair detector, it will just tell you the location of the chair in a given image. It will not tell you whether it's a red chair with a high back or a blue chair with a low back. Detecting the location of objects is a very critical step in many Computer Vision systems. Consider the following image:

If you run a chair detector on this image, it will put a green box around all the chairs. It won't tell you what kind of chair it is! Object detection used to be a computationally intensive task because of the number of calculations required to perform the detection at various scales. To solve this, Paul Viola and Michael Jones came up with a great algorithm in their seminal paper in 2001. You can read it at `https://www.cs.cmu.edu/~efros/courses/LBMV07/Papers/viola-cvpr-01.pdf`. They provided a fast way to design an object detector for any object. OpenCV has modules called `objdetect` and `xobjdetect` that provide the framework to design an object detector. You can use it to develop detectors for random items such as sunglasses, boots, and so on.

Machine learning

Computer Vision uses various machine learning algorithms to achieve different things. OpenCV provides a module called `ml` that has many machine learning algorithms bundled into it. Some of the algorithms include Bayes Classifier, K-Nearest Neighbors, Support Vector Machines, Decision Trees, Neural Networks, and so on. It also has a module called `flann` that contains algorithms for fast-nearest-neighbor searches in large datasets. Machine learning algorithms are used extensively to build systems for object recognition, image classification, face detection, visual searches, and so on.

Computational photography

Computational photography refers to using advanced image processing techniques to improve the images captured by cameras. Instead of focusing on optical processes and image capture methods, computational photography uses software to manipulate visual data. Some applications include high dynamic range imaging, panoramic images, image relighting, light field cameras, and so on.

Downloading the example code

You can download the example code files for all Packt books you have purchased from your account at `http://www.packtpub.com`. If you purchased this book elsewhere, you can visit `http://www.packtpub.com/support` and register to have the files e-mailed directly to you. Instructions for running example are available in the `README.md` file present in the root folder of each project.

Let's take a look at the following image:

Look at those vivid colors! This is an example of a high dynamic range image and it wouldn't be possible to get this using conventional image capture techniques. To do this, we have to capture the same scene at multiple exposures, register those images with each other, and then blend them nicely to create this image. The photo and xphoto modules contain various algorithms that provide algorithms pertaining to computational photography. There is a module called stitching that provides algorithms to create panoramic images.

 The preceding image can be found at https://pixabay.com/en/ hdr-high-dynamic-range-landscape-806260/.

Shape analysis

The notion of shape is crucial in Computer Vision. We analyze the visual data by recognizing various different shapes in the image. This is actually an important step in many algorithms. Let's say you are trying to identify a particular logo in an image. Now, you know that it can appear in various shapes, orientations, sizes, and so on. One good way to get started is to quantify the characteristics of the shape of the object. The module `shape` provides all the algorithms required to extract different shapes, measure similarities between them, transform shapes of objects, and so on.

Optical flow algorithms

Optical flow algorithms are used in videos to track features across successive frames. Let's say you want to track a particular object in a video. Running a feature extractor on each frame would be computationally expensive; hence, the process would be slow. So, you just need to extract the features from the current frame and then track these features in successive frames. Optical flow algorithms are heavily used in video-based applications in Computer Vision. The `optflow` module contains a number of algorithms required to perform optical flow. There is also a module called `tracking` that contains more algorithms that can be used to track features.

Face and object recognition

Face recognition refers to identifying the person in a given image. This is not the same as face detection where you identify the location of a face in the given image. So, if you want to build a practical biometric system that can recognize the person in front of the camera, you first need to run the face detector that can identify the location of the face, and then, run a face recognizer that can recognize who that person is. There is a module called `face` that deals with face recognition.

As discussed earlier, Computer Vision tries to model algorithms based on how humans perceive the visual data. So, it would be helpful to find salient regions and objects in the images that can help different applications, such as object recognition, object detection and tracking, and so on. There is a module called `saliency` that's designed for this purpose. It provides algorithms that can detect salient regions in static images and videos.

Surface matching

We are increasingly interacting with devices that can capture the 3D structure of the objects around us. These devices basically capture the depth information along with the regular 2D color images. So, it's important for us to build algorithms that can understand and process 3D objects. Kinect is a good example of a device that captures the depth information along with the visual data. The task at hand is to recognize the input 3D object by matching it with one of the models in our database. If we have a system that can recognize and locate objects, then it can be used for many different applications. There is a module called surface_matching that contains algorithms for 3D object recognition and a pose estimation algorithm using 3D features.

Text detection and recognition

Identifying text in a given scene and recognizing the content is becoming increasingly important. Some applications include nameplate recognition, recognizing road signs for self-driving cars, book scanning to digitize the contents, and so on. There is a module called text that contains various algorithms to handle text detection and recognition.

Installing OpenCV

Let's see how to get OpenCV up-and-running on various operating systems.

Windows

To keep things easy, let's install OpenCV using prebuilt libraries. Let's go to http://opencv.org and download the latest version for Windows. The current version is 3.0.0, and you can go to the OpenCV homepage to get the latest link to download the package.

You need to make sure you have admin rights before you proceed. The downloaded file will be an executable file, so just double-click on it to start the installation process. The installer expands the content into a folder. You will be able to choose the installation path and check the installation by inspecting the files.

Once you are done with the previous step, we need to set the OpenCV environment variables and add it to the system path to complete the installation. We will set up an environment variable that will hold the build directory of the OpenCV library. We will be using this in our projects. Open the terminal and type the following command:

```
C:\> setx -m OPENCV_DIR D:\OpenCV\Build\x64\vc11
```

> We are assuming that you have a 64-bit machine with Visual Studio 2012 installed. If you have Visual Studio 2010, replace vc11 with vc10 in the preceding command. The path specified earlier is where we will have our OpenCV binaries, and you will see two folders inside this path called lib and bin. If you are using Visual Studio 2015, you should be able to compile OpenCV from scratch.

Let's go ahead and add the path to the bin folder of our system's path. The reason we need to do this is because we will be using the OpenCV library in the form of **Dynamic Link Libraries (DLLs)**. Basically, all the OpenCV algorithms are stored here, and our operating system will only load them during runtime. In order to do this, our operating system needs to know where they are located. The system's PATH variable will contain a list of all the folders where it can find the DLLs. So, naturally, we need to add the path to the OpenCV library to this list. Now, why do we need to do all this? Well, the other option is to copy the required DLLs to the same folder as the application's executable file (the .exe file). This is an unnecessary overhead, especially when we are working with many different projects.

We need to edit the PATH variable in order to add it to this folder. You can use software such as Path Editor to do this. You can download it from https://patheditor2.codeplex.com. Once you install it, start it and add the following new entry (you can right-click on the path to insert a new item):

```
%OPENCV_DIR%\bin
```

Go ahead and save it to the registry. We are done!

Mac OS X

In this section, we will see how to install OpenCV on Mac OS X. Precompiled binaries are not available for Mac OS X, so we need to compile OpenCV from scratch. Before we proceed, we need to install CMake. If you don't have CMake already installed, you can download it from https://cmake.org/files/v3.3/cmake-3.3.2-Darwin-x86_64.dmg. It's a DMG file! So, once you download it, just run the installer.

Download the latest version of OpenCV from opencv.org. The current version is 3.0.0, and you can download it from `https://github.com/Itseez/opencv/archive/3.0.0.zip`.

Unzip the contents into a folder of your choice. OpenCV 3.0.0 also has a new package called `opencv_contrib` that contains user contributions that are not yet considered stable. One thing to keep in mind is that some of the algorithms in the `opencv_contrib` package are not freely available for commercial use. Also, installing this package is optional. OpenCV will work just fine if you don't install `opencv_contrib`. Since we are installing OpenCV anyway, it's good to install this package so that you can experiment with it later on (as opposed to going through the whole installation process again). This package is a great way to learn and play around with new algorithms. You can download it from `https://github.com/Itseez/opencv_contrib/archive/3.0.0.zip`.

Unzip the contents of the ZIP file into a folder of your choice. For convenience, unzip it into the same folder, as mentioned earlier, so that the `opencv-3.0.0` and `opencv_contrib-3.0.0` folders are in the same main folder.

We are now ready to build OpenCV. Open your terminal and navigate to the folder where you unzipped the contents of OpenCV 3.0.0. Run the following commands after substituting the right paths in the commands:

```
$ cd /full/path/to/opencv-3.0.0/
$ mkdir build
$ cd build
$ cmake -D CMAKE_BUILD_TYPE=RELEASE -D CMAKE_INSTALL_PREFIX=/full/path/to/opencv-3.0.0/build -D INSTALL_C_EXAMPLES=ON -D BUILD_EXAMPLES=ON -D OPENCV_EXTRA_MODULES_PATH=/full/path/to/opencv_contrib-3.0.0/modules ../
```

It's time to install OpenCV 3.0.0. Go inside the `/full/path/to/opencv-3.0.0/build` directory and run the following commands on your terminal:

```
$ make -j4
$ make install
```

In the preceding command, the `-j4` flag indicates that it is using four cores to install it. It's faster this way! Now, let's set the library path. Open your `~/.profile` file in your terminal using the `vi ~/.profile` command, and add the following line:

```
export DYLD_LIBRARY_PATH=/full/path/to/opencv-3.0.0/build/lib:$DYLD_LIBRARY_PATH
```

We need to copy the `pkg-config` file `opencv.pc` to `/usr/local/lib/pkgconfig` and name it `opencv3.pc`. This way, if you already have an existing `OpenCV 2.4.x` installation, there will be no conflicts. Let's go ahead and do this:

```
$ cp /full/path/to/opencv-3.0.0/build/lib/pkgconfig/opencv.pc /usr/local/
lib/pkgconfig/opencv3.pc
```

We need to update our `PKG_CONFIG_PATH` variable as well. Open your `~/.profile` file, and add the following line:

```
    export PKG_CONFIG_PATH=/usr/local/lib/pkgconfig/:$PKG_CONFIG_PATH
```

Reload your `~/.profile` file using the following command:

```
$ source ~/.profile
```

We are done! Let's see if it's working:

```
$ cd /full/path/to/opencv-3.0.0/samples/cpp
```

```
$ g++ -ggdb 'pkg-config --cflags --libs opencv3' opencv_version.cpp -o /
tmp/opencv_version && /tmp/opencv_version
```

If you see `Welcome to OpenCV 3.0.0` printed on your terminal, you are good to go. We will be using CMake to build our OpenCV projects throughout this book. We will cover this in more detail in the next chapter.

Linux

Let's see how to install OpenCV on Ubuntu. We need to install some dependencies before we begin. Let's install them using the package manager by running the following command on your terminal:

```
$ sudo apt-get -y install libopencv-dev build-essential cmake
libdc1394-22 libdc1394-22-dev libjpeg-dev libpng12-dev libtiff4-dev
libjasper-dev libavcodec-dev libavformat-dev libswscale-dev libxine-dev
libgstreamer0.10-dev libgstreamer-plugins-base0.10-dev libv4l-dev libtbb-
dev libqt4-dev libmp3lame-dev libopencore-amrnb-dev libopencore-amrwb-dev
libtheora-dev libvorbis-dev libxvidcore-dev x264 v4l-utils
```

Now that you have installed the dependencies, let's download, build, and install OpenCV:

```
$ wget "https://github.com/Itseez/opencv/archive/3.0.0.zip" -O opencv.zip
```

```
$ wget "https://github.com/Itseez/opencv_contrib/archive/3.0.0.zip" -O
opencv_contrib.zip
```

```
$ unzip opencv.zip -d .
```

```
$ unzip opencv_contrib.zip -d .
```

```
$ cd opencv-3.0.0
```

```
$ mkdir build
```

```
$ cd build
```

```
$ cmake -D CMAKE_BUILD_TYPE=RELEASE -D CMAKE_INSTALL_PREFIX=/full/path/
to/opencv-3.0.0/build -D INSTALL_C_EXAMPLES=ON -D BUILD_EXAMPLES=ON -D
OPENCV_EXTRA_MODULES_PATH=/full/path/to/opencv_contrib-3.0.0/modules ../
```

```
$ make -j4
```

```
$ sudo make install
```

Let's copy the `pkg-config` file's `opencv.pc` to `/usr/local/lib/pkgconfig` and name it `opencv3.pc`:

```
$ cp /full/path/to/opencv-3.0.0/build/lib/pkgconfig/opencv.pc /usr/local/
lib/pkgconfig/opencv3.pc
```

We are done! We will now be able to use it to compile our OpenCV programs from the command line. Also, if you already have an existing OpenCV 2.4.x installation, there will be no conflicts. Let's check whether the installation is working properly:

```
$ cd /full/path/to/opencv-3.0.0/samples/cpp
```

```
$ g++ -ggdb 'pkg-config --cflags --libs opencv3' opencv_version.cpp -o /
tmp/opencv_version && /tmp/opencv_version
```

If you see `Welcome to OpenCV 3.0.0` printed on your terminal, you are good to go. In the following chapters, you will learn how to use CMake to build your OpenCV projects.

Summary

In this chapter, we learned how to install OpenCV across various operating systems. We discussed the human visual system and how humans process visual data. We understood why it's difficult for machines to do the same and what we need to consider while designing a Computer Vision library. We learned what can be done using OpenCV and the various modules that can be used to do those tasks.

In the next chapter, we will discuss how to operate on images and how we can manipulate them using various functions. We will also learn how to build a project structure for our OpenCV applications.

2
An Introduction to the Basics of OpenCV

After covering the installation of OpenCV on different operating systems in *Chapter 1*, *Getting Started with OpenCV*, we are going to introduce the basics of OpenCV development in this chapter.

In this chapter, you will learn how to create your project using CMake.

We will also introduce the image basic data structures, matrices, and other structures that are required in our projects.

We will learn how to save our variables and data in files using the XML/YAML persistence OpenCV functions.

In this chapter, we will cover the following topics:

- Configuring projects with CMake
- Reading/writing images from/to disk
- Reading videos and accessing camera devices
- The main image structures (matrices)
- Other important and basic structures (vectors, scalars, and so on)
- An introduction to basic matrix operations
- File storage operations with the XML/YAML persistence OpenCV API

Basic CMake configuration files

To configure and check all the required dependencies of our project, we are going to use CMake; but it is not mandatory, so we can configure our project in any other tool or IDE such as Makefiles or Visual Studio. However, CMake is the most portable way to configure multiplatform C++ projects.

CMake uses configuration files called CMakeLists.txt, where the compilation and dependency processes are defined. For a basic project, based on an executable build from one source code file, a two-line CMakeLists.txt file is all that is needed. The file looks like this:

```
cmake_minimum_required (VERSION 2.6)
project (CMakeTest)
add_executable(${PROJECT_NAME} main.cpp)
```

The first line defines the minimum version of CMake required. This line is mandatory in our CMakeLists.txt file and allows you to use the cmake functionality defined from a given version defined in the second line; it defines the project name. This name is saved in a variable called PROJECT_NAME.

The last line creates an executable command (add_executable()) in the main.cpp file, gives it the same name as our project (${PROJECT_NAME}), and compiles our source code into an executable called CMakeTest, which we set as the project name.

The ${} expression allows access to any variable defined in our environment. Then, we can use the ${PROJECT_NAME} variable as an executable output name.

Creating a library

CMake allows you to create libraries, which are indeed used by the OpenCV build system. Factorizing the shared code among multiple applications is a common and useful practice in software development. In big applications or when the common code is shared in multiple applications, this practice is very useful.

In this case, we do not create a binary executable; instead, we create a compiled file that includes all the functions, classes, and so on, developed. We can then share this library file with the other applications without sharing our source code.

CMake includes the add_library function for this purpose:

```
# Create our hello library
add_library(Hello hello.cpp hello.h)
```

```
# Create our application that uses our new library
add_executable(executable main.cpp)

# Link our executable with the new library
target_link_libraries( executable Hello )
```

The lines starting with # add comments and are ignored by CMake.

The `add_library(Hello hello.cpp hello.h)` command defines our new library called, where `Hello` is the library name and `hello.cpp`, `hello.h` are the source files. We add the header file to allow IDEs such as Visual Studio to link to the header files.

This line will generate a shared file (So for OS X and Unix or .dll for Windows) or a static library (A for OS X and Unix or .dll for Windows), depending on our operating system or if it is a dynamic or static library.

`target_link_libraries( executable Hello)` is the function that links our executable to the desired library; in our case, it's the `Hello` library.

Managing dependencies

CMake has the ability to search our dependencies and external libraries, giving us the facility to build complex projects depending on external components in our projects and by adding some requirements.

In this book, the most important dependency is, of course, OpenCV, and we will add it to all our projects:

```
cmake_minimum_required (VERSION 2.6)
cmake_policy(SET CMP0012 NEW)
PROJECT(Chapter2)
# Requires OpenCV
FIND_PACKAGE( OpenCV 3.0.0 REQUIRED )
# Show a message with the opencv version detected
MESSAGE("OpenCV version : ${OpenCV_VERSION}")
include_directories(${OpenCV_INCLUDE_DIRS})
link_directories(${OpenCV_LIB_DIR})
# Create a variable called SRC
SET(SRC main.cpp )
# Create our executable
ADD_EXECUTABLE( ${PROJECT_NAME} ${SRC} )
# Link our library
TARGET_LINK_LIBRARIES( ${PROJECT_NAME} ${OpenCV_LIBS} )
```

Now, let's understand the working of the script:

```
cmake_minimum_required (VERSION 2.6)
cmake_policy(SET CMP0012 NEW)
PROJECT(Chapter2)
```

The first line defines the minimum CMake version; the second line tells CMake to use the new behavior of CMake so that it can correctly recognize numbers and Booleans constants without dereferencing variables with such names. This policy was introduced in CMake 2.8.0, and CMake warns when the policy is not set to version 3.0.2. Finally, the last line defines the project title:

```
# Requires OpenCV
FIND_PACKAGE( OpenCV 3.0.0 REQUIRED )
# Show a message with the opencv version detected
MESSAGE("OpenCV version : ${OpenCV_VERSION}")
include_directories(${OpenCV_INCLUDE_DIRS})
link_directories(${OpenCV_LIB_DIR})
```

This is where we search for our OpenCV dependency. FIND_PACKAGE is the function that allows us to find our dependencies and the minimum version required if this dependency is required or optional. In this sample script, we look for OpenCV in version 3.0.0 or greater and it is a required package.

> The FIND_PACKAGE command includes all OpenCV submodules, but you can specify the submodules that you want to include in the project by making your application smaller and faster. For example, if we are going to work only with the basic OpenCV types and core functionalities, we can use the following command:
>
> **FIND_PACKAGE(OpenCV 3.0.0 REQUIRED core)**

If CMake does not find it, it returns an error and does not prevent us from compiling our application.

The MESSAGE function shows a message on the terminal or CMake GUI. In our case, we will show the OpenCV version, as follows:

```
OpenCV version : 3.0.0
```

${OpenCV_VERSION} is a variable where CMake stores the OpenCV package version.

The include_directories() and link_directories() add the header and the directory of the specified library to our environment. OpenCV's CMake module saves this data in the ${OpenCV_INCLUDE_DIRS} and ${OpenCV_LIB_DIR} variables. These lines are not required in all platforms, such as Linux, because these paths are normally in the environment, but it's recommended that you have more than one OpenCV version to choose from the correct link and include directories:

```
# Create a variable called SRC
SET(SRC main.cpp )
# Create our executable
ADD_EXECUTABLE( ${PROJECT_NAME} ${SRC} )
# Link our library
TARGET_LINK_LIBRARIES( ${PROJECT_NAME} ${OpenCV_LIBS} )
```

This last line creates the executable and links it to the OpenCV library, as we saw in the previous section, *Creating a library*.

There is a new function in this piece of code called SET. This function creates a new variable and adds any value that we need to it. In our case, we set the SRC variable to the main.cpp value. However, we can add more and more values to the same variable, as shown in this script:

```
SET(SRC main.cpp
        utils.cpp
        color.cpp
)
```

Making the script more complex

In this section, we will show you a more complex script that includes subfolders, libraries, and executables, all in only two files and a few lines, as shown in this script.

It's not mandatory to create multiple CMakeLists.txt files because we can specify everything in the main CMakeLists.txt file. It is more common to use different CMakeLists.txt files for each project subfolder, making it more flexible and portable.

This example has a code structure folder that contains one folder for the utils library and the other for the root folder, which contains the main executable:

```
CMakeLists.txt
main.cpp
utils/
   CMakeLists.txt
   computeTime.cpp
   computeTime.h
   logger.cpp
   logger.h
   plotting.cpp
   plotting.h
```

Then, we need to define two CMakeLists.txt files: one in the root folder and the other in the utils folder. The CMakeLists.txt root folder file has the following contents:

```
cmake_minimum_required (VERSION 2.6)
project (Chapter2)

# Opencv Package required
FIND_PACKAGE( OpenCV  3.0.0 REQUIRED )

#Add opencv header files to project
include_directories( ${OpenCV_INCLUDE_DIR} )
link_directories(${OpenCV_LIB_DIR})

add_subdirectory(utils)


# Add optional log with a precompiler definition
option(WITH_LOG "Build with output logs and images in tmp" OFF)
if(WITH_LOG)
   add_definitions(-DLOG)
endif(WITH_LOG)

# generate our new executable
add_executable( ${PROJECT_NAME} main.cpp )
# link the project with his dependencies
target_link_libraries( ${PROJECT_NAME} ${OpenCV_LIBS} Utils)
```

Almost all the lines are described in the previous sections except for some functions that we will explain in later sections.

The `add_subdirectory()` tells CMake to analyze the `CMakeLists.txt` of a desired subfolder.

Before we continue with an explanation of the main `CMakeLists.txt` file, we will explain the `utils` `CMakeLists.txt` file.

In the `CMakeLists.txt` file in the `utils` folder, we will write a new library to include it in our main project folder:

```
# Add new variable for src utils lib
SET(UTILS_LIB_SRC
  computeTime.cpp
  logger.cpp
  plotting.cpp
)
# create our new utils lib
add_library(Utils ${UTILS_LIB_SRC} )
# make sure the compiler can find include files for our library
target_include_directories(Utils PUBLIC ${CMAKE_CURRENT_SOURCE_DIR})
```

This CMake script file defines an `UTILS_LIB_SRC` variable where we add all the source files included in our library, generate the library with the `add_library` function, and use the `target_include_directories` function to allow our main project to detect all header files.

Leaving out the `utils` subfolder and continuing with the root `cmake` script, the Option function creates a new variable—in our case, `WITH_LOG`, with a small description attached. This variable can be changed via the `ccmake` command line or CMake GUI interface, where the description and a checkbox appears that allow users to enable or disable this option.

This function is very useful and allows the user to decide about compile-time features such as enabling or disabling logs, compiling with Java or Python support as with OpenCV, and so on.

In our case, we use this option to enable a logger in our application. To enable the logger, we use a precompiler definition in our code:

```
#ifdef LOG
logi("Number of iteration %d", i);
#endif
```

To tell our compiler that we require the LOG compile time definition, we use the add_definitions(-DLOG) function in our CMakeLists.txt. To allow the user to decide whether they want to enable it or not, we only have to verify whether the WITH_LOG CMake variable is checked or not with a simple condition:

```
if(WITH_LOG)
    add_definitions(-DLOG)
endif(WITH_LOG)
```

Now, we are ready to create our CMake script files to be compiled in any operating system our Computer Vision projects. Then, we will continue with the OpenCV basics before we start with a sample project.

Images and matrices

The most important structure in a Computer Vision is without any doubt the images. The image in Computer Vision is a representation of the physical world captured with a digital device. This picture is only a sequence of numbers stored in a matrix format, as shown in the following image. Each number is a measurement of the light intensity for the considered wavelength (for example, red, green, or blue in color images) or for a wavelength range (for panchromatic devices). Each point in an image is called a pixel (for a picture element), and each pixel can store one or more values depending on whether it is a gray, black, or white image (called a binary image as well) that stores only one value, such as 0 or 1, a gray-scale-level image that can store only one value, or a color image that can store three values. These values are usually integer numbers between 0 and 255, but you can use the other range. For example, 0 to 1 in a floating point numbers such as **HDRI (High Dynamic Range Imaging)** or thermal images.

The image is stored in a matrix format, where each pixel has a position in it and can be referenced by the number of the column and row. OpenCV uses the `Mat` class for this purpose. In the case of a grayscale image, a single matrix is used, as shown in the following figure:

159	165	185	187	185	190	189	198	193	197	184	152	123
174	167	186	194	185	196	204	191	200	178	149	129	125
168	184	185	188	195	192	191	195	169	141	116	115	129
178	188	190	195	196	199	195	164	128	120	118	126	135
188	194	189	195	201	196	166	114	113	120	128	131	129
187	200	197	198	190	144	107	106	113	120	125	125	125
198	195	202	183	134	98	97	112	114	115	116	116	118
194	206	178	111	87	99	97	101	107	105	101	97	95
206	168	107	82	80	100	102	91	98	102	104	99	72
160	97	80	86	80	92	80	79	71	74	81	81	64
98	66	76	86	78	83	72	71	65	53	61	61	56
60	76	74	70	67	64	63	60	55	49	54	52	54

In the case of a color image, as shown in the following image, we use a matrix of size width x height x number of colors:

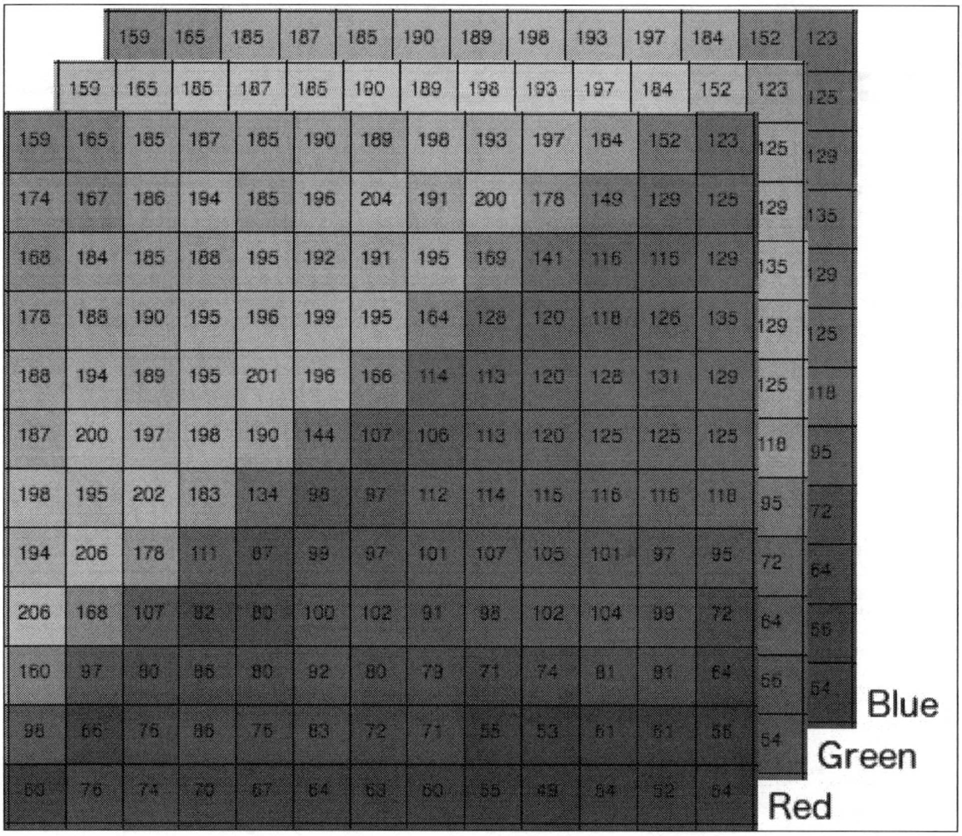

The Mat class is not only used to store images, but also to store different types of arbitrarily sized matrices. You can use is it as an algebraic matrix and perform operations with it. In the next section, we are going to describe the most important matrix operations such as add, matrix multiplication, create a diagonal matrix, and so on.

However, before that, it's important to know how the matrix is stored internally in the computer memory because it is always better to have efficient access to the memory slots instead of access to each pixel with the OpenCV functions.

In memory, the matrix is saved as an array or sequence of values ordered by columns and rows. The following table shows the sequence of pixels in the BGR image format:

Row 0									Row 1									Row 2								
Col 0			Col 1			Col 2			Col 0			Col 1			Col 2			Col 0			Col 1			Col 2		
Pixel 1			Pixel 2			Pixel 3			Pixel 4			Pixel 5			Pixel 6			Pixel 7			Pixel 8			Pixel 9		
B	G	R	B	G	R	B	G	R	B	G	R	B	G	R	B	G	R	B	G	R	B	G	R	B	G	R

With this order, we can access any pixel, as shown in the following formula:

```
Value= Row_i*num_cols*num_channels + Col_i + channel_i
```

 OpenCV functions are quite optimized for random access, but sometimes direct access to the memory (working with pointer arithmetic) is more efficient—for example, when we have access to all the pixels in a loop.

Reading/writing images

After the introduction of this matrix, we are going to start with the basics of the OpenCV code. Firstly, we need to learn how to read and write images:

```cpp
#include <iostream>
#include <string>
#include <sstream>
using namespace std;

// OpenCV includes
#include "opencv2/core.hpp"
#include "opencv2/highgui.hpp"
using namespace cv;

int main( int argc, const char** argv )
{
  // Read images
  Mat color= imread("../lena.jpg");
  Mat gray= imread("../lena.jpg", 0);

  // Write images
  imwrite("lenaGray.jpg", gray);
```

```
// Get same pixel with opencv function
int myRow=color.cols-1;
int myCol=color.rows-1;
Vec3b pixel= color.at<Vec3b>(myRow, myCol);
cout << "Pixel value (B,G,R): (" << (int)pixel[0] << "," <<
    (int)pixel[1] << "," << (int)pixel[2] << ")" << endl;

// show images
imshow("Lena BGR", color);
imshow("Lena Gray", gray);
// wait for any key press
waitKey(0);
return 0;
}
```

Let's try to understand this code:

```
// OpenCV includes
#include "opencv2/core.hpp"
#include "opencv2/highgui.hpp"
using namespace cv;
```

First, we have to include the declarations of the functions that we need in our sample. These functions come from core (basic image data handling) and high-gui (the cross-platform I/O functions provided by OpenCV are `core` and `highui`. The first includes the basic classes, such as matrices, and the second includes the functions to read, write, and show images with graphical interfaces).

```
// Read images
Mat color= imread("../lena.jpg");
Mat gray= imread("../lena.jpg", 0);
```

The **imread** is the main function used to read images. This function opens an image and stores the image in a matrix format. The `imread` function accepts two parameters: the first parameter is a string that contains the image's path, and the second parameter is optional and, by default, loads the image as a color image. The second parameter allows the following options:

- CV_LOAD_IMAGE_ANYDEPTH: If set to this constant, returns a 16-bit/32-bit image when the input has the corresponding depth; otherwise, the `imread` function converts it to an 8-bit image

- CV_LOAD_IMAGE_COLOR: If set to this constant, always converts the image to color

- CV_LOAD_IMAGE_GRAYSCALE: If set to this constant, always converts the image to grayscale

To save images, we can use the `imwrite` function, which stores a matrix image in our computer:

```
// Write images
imwrite("lenaGray.jpg", gray);
```

The first parameter is the path where we want to save the image with the extension format that we desire. The second parameter is the matrix image that we want to save. In our code sample, we create and store a gray version of the image and then save it as a JPG file the gray image that we loaded and store in `gray` variable:

```
// Get same pixel with opencv function
int myRow=color.cols-1;
int myCol=color.rows-1;
```

Using the `.cols` and `.rows` attributes of a matrix, we can access the number of columns and rows of an image — or in other words, the width and height:

```
Vec3b pixel= color.at<Vec3b>(myRow, myCol);
cout << "Pixel value (B,G,R): (" << (int)pixel[0] << "," << (int)
pixel[1] << "," << (int)pixel[2] << ")" << endl;
```

To access one pixel of an image, we use the `cv::Mat::at<typename t>(row,col)` template function from the `Mat` OpenCV class. The template parameter is the desired return type. A `typename` in an 8-bit color image is a `Vec3b` class that stores three unsigned char data (Vec=vector, 3=number of components, and b = 1 byte). In the case of the gray image, we can directly use the unsigned char or any other number format used in the image, such as `uchar pixel= color.at<uchar>(myRow, myCol)`:

```
// show images
imshow("Lena BGR", color);
imshow("Lena Gray", gray);
// wait for any key press
waitKey(0);
```

Finally, to show the images, we can use the `imshow` function that creates a window with a title as the first parameter and the image matrix as the second parameter.

 If we want to stop our application by waiting for the user to press a key, we can use the OpenCV `waitKey` function with a parameter set to the number of milliseconds we want to wait. If we set the parameter to `0`, then the function will wait forever.

The result of this code is shown in the following picture; the left-hand image is a color image and right-hand image is a gray scale:

Finally, as an example for the following samples, we are going to create the CMakeLists.txt to allow you to compile our project and also see how to compile it.

The following code describes the CMakeLists.txt file:

```
cmake_minimum_required (VERSION 2.6)
cmake_policy(SET CMP0012 NEW)
PROJECT(project)

# Requires OpenCV
FIND_PACKAGE( OpenCV 3.0.0 REQUIRED )
MESSAGE("OpenCV version : ${OpenCV_VERSION}")

include_directories(${OpenCV_INCLUDE_DIRS})
link_directories(${OpenCV_LIB_DIR})
ADD_EXECUTABLE( sample main.cpp )
TARGET_LINK_LIBRARIES( sample ${OpenCV_LIBS} )
```

To compile our code, using the `CMakeLists.txt` file we have to perform the following steps:

1. Create a `build` folder.

2. Inside the `build` folder, execute `cmake` or open the `CMake gui` app in Windows, choose the source folder and build folder, and click on the Configure and Generate buttons.

3. After step 2, if we are in Linux or OS, generate a `makefile`; then we have to compile the project using the make command. If we are in Windows, we have to open the project with the editor that we selected in step 2 and compile it.

4. After step 3, we have an executable called `app`.

Reading videos and cameras

This section introduces you to reading a video and camera with this simple example:

```cpp
#include <iostream>
#include <string>
#include <sstream>
using namespace std;

// OpenCV includes
#include "opencv2/core.hpp"
#include "opencv2/highgui.hpp"
using namespace cv;

// OpenCV command line parser functions
// Keys accecpted by command line parser
const char* keys =
{
    "{help h usage ? | | print this message}"
    "{@video | | Video file, if not defined try to use webcamera}"
};

int main( int argc, const char** argv )
{
    CommandLineParser parser(argc, argv, keys);
    parser.about("Chapter 2. v1.0.0");
```

```
//If requires help show
if (parser.has("help"))
{
  parser.printMessage();
  return 0;
}
String videoFile= parser.get<String>(0);

// Check if params are correctly parsed in his variables
if (!parser.check())
{
    parser.printErrors();
    return 0;
}

VideoCapture cap; // open the default camera
if(videoFile != "")
    cap.open(videoFile);
else
    cap.open(0);
if(!cap.isOpened())  // check if we succeeded
    return -1;

namedWindow("Video",1);
for(;;)
{
    Mat frame;
    cap >> frame; // get a new frame from camera
    imshow("Video", frame);
    if(waitKey(30) >= 0) break;
}
// Release the camera or video cap
cap.release();

return 0;
}
```

Before we explain how to read video or camera inputs, we need to introduce a useful new class that will help us manage the input command line parameters; this new class was introduced in OpenCV version 3.0 and is called the `CommandLineParser` class:

```
// OpenCV command line parser functions
// Keys accepted by command line parser
const char* keys =
{
    "{help h usage ? | | print this message}"
    "{@video | | Video file, if not defined try to use webcamera}"
};
```

The first thing that we have to do for a command-line parser is define the parameters that we need or allow in a constant char vector; each line has this pattern:

```
{ name_param | default_value | description}
```

The `name_param` can be preceded with @, which defines this parameter as a default input. We can use more than one `name_param`:

```
CommandLineParser parser(argc, argv, keys);
```

The constructor will get the inputs of the main function and the key constants defined previously:

```
//If requires help show
if (parser.has("help"))
{
        parser.printMessage();
        return 0;
}
```

The `.has` class method checks the parameter's existence. In this sample, we check whether the user has added the `-help` or `?` parameter, and then, use the `printMessage` class function to show all the description parameters:

```
String videoFile= parser.get<String>(0);
```

With the `.get<typename>(parameterName)` function, we can access and read any of the input parameters:

```
// Check if params are correctly parsed in his variables
if (!parser.check())
{
    parser.printErrors();
    return 0;
}
```

After getting all the required parameters, we can check whether these parameters are parsed correctly and show an error message if one of the parameters is not parsed. For example, add a string instead of a number:

```
VideoCapture cap; // open the default camera
if(videoFile != "")
    cap.open(videoFile);
    else
    cap.open(0);
    if(!cap.isOpened())  // check if we succeeded
    return -1;
```

The class to read a video and camera is the same. The `VideoCapture` class belongs to the `videoio` submodel instead of the `highgui` submodule, as in the former version of OpenCV. After creating the object, we check whether the input command line `videoFile` parameter has a path filename. If it's empty, then we try to open a web camera and, if it has a filename, then we open the video file. To do this, we use the open function, giving the video filename or the index camera that we want to open as a parameter. If we have a single camera, we can use 0 as a parameter.

To check whether we can read the video filename or the camera, we use the `isOpened` function:

```
namedWindow("Video",1);
for(;;)
{
    Mat frame;
    cap >> frame; // get a new frame from camera
     if(frame)
        imshow("Video", frame);
    if(waitKey(30) >= 0) break;
}
// Release the camera or video cap
cap.release();
```

Finally, we create a window to show the frames with the `namedWindow` function and, with a non-finish loop, we grab each frame with the `>>` operation and show the image with the `imshow` function, if we correctly retrieve the frame. In this case, we don't want to stop the application, but we want to wait for 30 milliseconds to check whether users want to stop the application execution with any key using `waitKey(30)`.

> To choose a good value to wait for the next frame, using a camera access is calculated from the speed of the camera. For example, if a camera works at 20 FPS, a great wait value is *40 = 1000/20*.

When the user wants to finish the app, he has to only press a key, and then we have to release all the video resources using the `release` function.

> It is very important to release all the resources that we use in a Computer Vision application; if we do not do it, we can consume all the RAM memory. We can release the matrices with the `release` function.

The result of the code is a new window that shows a video or web camera in the BGR format, as shown in the following screenshot:

Other basic object types

We have learned about the Mat and Vec3b classes, but we need to learn about other classes as well.

In this section, we will learn about the most basic object types required in most of the projects:

- Vec
- Scalar
- Point
- Size
- Rect
- RotatedRect

The vec object type

vec is a template class that is used mainly for numerical vectors. We can define any type of vectors and a number of components:

```
Vec<double,19> myVector;
```

Or we can use any of the predefined types:

```
typedef Vec<uchar, 2> Vec2b;
typedef Vec<uchar, 3> Vec3b;
typedef Vec<uchar, 4> Vec4b;

typedef Vec<short, 2> Vec2s;
typedef Vec<short, 3> Vec3s;
typedef Vec<short, 4> Vec4s;

typedef Vec<int, 2> Vec2i;
typedef Vec<int, 3> Vec3i;
typedef Vec<int, 4> Vec4i;

typedef Vec<float, 2> Vec2f;
typedef Vec<float, 3> Vec3f;
typedef Vec<float, 4> Vec4f;
typedef Vec<float, 6> Vec6f;
```

```
typedef Vec<double, 2> Vec2d;
typedef Vec<double, 3> Vec3d;
typedef Vec<double, 4> Vec4d;
typedef Vec<double, 6> Vec6d;
```

All the expected vector operations are also implemented, as follows:

```
v1 = v2 + v3
v1 = v2 - v3
v1 = v2 * scale
v1 = scale * v2
v1 = -v2
```
v1 += v2 and other augmenting operations
```
v1 == v2, v1 != v2
norm(v1) (euclidean norm)
```

The Scalar object type

The Scalar object type is a template class derived from Vec with four elements. The Scalar type is widely used in OpenCV to pass and read pixel values.

To access the values of Vec and Scalar, we use the [] operator.

The Point object type

Another very common class template is Point. This class defines a 2D point specified by its x and y coordinates.

> Like the Point object type, there is a Point3 template class for 3D point support.

Like the Vec class, OpenCV defines the following Point aliases for our convenience:

```
typedef Point_<int> Point2i;
typedef Point2i Point;
typedef Point_<float> Point2f;
typedef Point_<double> Point2d;
```

The following operators are defined for points:

```
pt1 = pt2 + pt3;
pt1 = pt2 - pt3;
pt1 = pt2 * a;
pt1 = a * pt2;
pt1 = pt2 / a;
pt1 += pt2;
pt1 -= pt2;
pt1 *= a;
pt1 /= a;
double value = norm(pt); // L2 norm
pt1 == pt2;
pt1 != pt2;
```

The Size object type

Another `template` class that is very important and used in OpenCV is the `template` class used to specify the size of an image or rectangle, Size. This class adds two members: the width and height and a useful `area()` function.

The Rect object type

`Rect` is another important template class used to define 2D rectangles by the following parameters:

- The coordinates of the top-left corner
- The width and height of a rectangle

The `Rect` template class can be used to define a **ROI (region of interest)** of an image.

RotatedRect object type

The last useful class is a particular rectangle called `RotatedRect`. This class represents a rotated rectangle specified by a center point, the width and height of a rectangle, and the rotation angle in degrees:

```
RotatedRect(const Point2f& center, const Size2f& size, float angle);
```

An interesting function of this class is `boundingBox`; this function returns a `Rect` that contains the rotated rectangle:

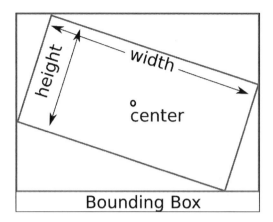

Basic matrix operations

In this section, we will learn some basic and important matrix operations that we can apply to images or any matrix data.

We learned how to load an image and store it in a `Mat` variable, but we can manually create a Mat variable. The most common constructor that provides the matrix size and type is as follows:

```
Mat a= Mat(Size(5,5), CV_32F);
```

 You can create a new `Matrix link` with a stored buffer from third-party libraries, without copying the data, using the following constructor:

```
Mat(size, type, pointer_to_buffer)
```

The supported types depend on the type of the number you want to store and the number of channels. The most common types are as follows:

```
CV_8UC1
CV_8UC3
CV_8UC4
CV_32FC1
CV_32FC3
CV_32FC4
```

You can create any type of a matrix using `CV_number_typeC(n)`, where `number_type` is 8U (8 bits unsigned) to 64F (64 float) and (n) is the number of channels. The number of channels allowed is from 1 to `CV_CN_MAX`.

This initialization does not set up the data values and you can get undesirable values. To avoid undesirable values, you can initialize the matrix with `zeros` or `ones` values with the `zeros` or `ones` function:

```
Mat mz= Mat::zeros(5,5, CV_32F);
Mat mo= Mat::ones(5,5, CV_32F);
```

The output of the preceding matrix is as follows:

$$\begin{bmatrix} 0 & 0 & 0 & 0 & 0 \\ 0 & 0 & 0 & 0 & 0 \\ 0 & 0 & 0 & 0 & 0 \\ 0 & 0 & 0 & 0 & 0 \\ 0 & 0 & 0 & 0 & 0 \end{bmatrix} \begin{bmatrix} 1 & 1 & 1 & 1 & 1 \\ 1 & 1 & 1 & 1 & 1 \\ 1 & 1 & 1 & 1 & 1 \\ 1 & 1 & 1 & 1 & 1 \\ 1 & 1 & 1 & 1 & 1 \end{bmatrix}$$

A special matrix initialization is the **eye** function that creates an `identity` matrix with the specified type (`CV_8UC1`, `CV_8UC3`...) and size:

```
Mat m= Mat::eye(5,5, CV_32F);
```

The output is as follows:

$$\begin{bmatrix} 1 & 0 & 0 & 0 & 0 \\ 0 & 1 & 0 & 0 & 0 \\ 0 & 0 & 1 & 0 & 0 \\ 0 & 0 & 0 & 1 & 0 \\ 0 & 0 & 0 & 0 & 1 \end{bmatrix}$$

All matrix operations are allowed in the OpenCV Mat class. We can add or subtract two matrices with + and - operators:

```
Mat a= Mat::eye(Size(3,2), CV_32F);
Mat b= Mat::ones(Size(3,2), CV_32F);
Mat c= a+b;
Mat d= a-b;
```

The results of the previous operations are as follows:

$$\begin{bmatrix} 1 & 0 & 0 \\ 0 & 1 & 0 \end{bmatrix} + \begin{bmatrix} 1 & 1 & 1 \\ 1 & 1 & 1 \end{bmatrix} = \begin{bmatrix} 2 & 1 & 1 \\ 1 & 2 & 1 \end{bmatrix}$$

$$\begin{bmatrix} 1 & 0 & 0 \\ 0 & 1 & 0 \end{bmatrix} - \begin{bmatrix} 1 & 1 & 1 \\ 1 & 1 & 1 \end{bmatrix} = \begin{bmatrix} 0 & -1 & -1 \\ -1 & 0 & -1 \end{bmatrix}$$

We can multiply a matrix by a scalar with the * operator, a matrix per element matrix with the `mul` function, or a matrix by matrix multiplication with * operator:

```
Mat m1= Mat::eye(2,3, CV_32F);
Mat m2= Mat::ones(3,2, CV_32F);
// Scalar by matrix
cout << "\nm1.*2\n" << m1*2 << endl;
// matrix per element multiplication
cout << "\n(m1+2).*(m1+3)\n" << (m1+1).mul(m1+3) << endl;
// Matrix multiplication
cout << "\nm1*m2\n" << m1*m2 << endl;
```

The results of the previous operations are as follows:

$$\begin{bmatrix} 1 & 0 & 0 \\ 0 & 1 & 0 \end{bmatrix} * 2 = \begin{bmatrix} 2 & 0 & 0 \\ 0 & 2 & 0 \end{bmatrix}$$

$$\begin{bmatrix} 2 & 1 & 1 \\ 1 & 2 & 1 \end{bmatrix} .* \begin{bmatrix} 4 & 3 & 3 \\ 3 & 4 & 3 \end{bmatrix} = \begin{bmatrix} 8 & 3 & 3 \\ 3 & 8 & 3 \end{bmatrix}$$

$$\begin{bmatrix} 1 & 0 & 0 \\ 0 & 1 & 0 \end{bmatrix} * \begin{bmatrix} 1 & 1 \\ 1 & 1 \\ 1 & 1 \end{bmatrix} = \begin{bmatrix} 1 & 1 \\ 1 & 1 \end{bmatrix}$$

The other common mathematical matrix operations are transposition and matrix inversion, defined by the t() and inv() functions, respectively.

Other interesting functions that OpenCV provides us with are array operations in a matrix; for example, count the non-zero elements. This is useful to count the pixels or area of an object:

```
int countNonZero( src );
```

OpenCV provides some statistical functions. The mean and standard deviation by channel can be calculated using the meanStdDev function:

```
meanStdDev(src, mean, stddev);
```

The other useful statistical function is minMaxLoc. This function finds the minimum and the maximum of a matrix or array and returns its location and value:

```
minMaxLoc(src, minVal, maxVal, minLoc, maxLoc);
```

Here, src is the input matrix, minVal and maxVal are double values detected, and minLoc and maxLoc are point values detected.

 Other core and useful functions are described in detail at http://docs.opencv.org/modules/core/doc/core.html.

Basic data persistence and storage

Before we finish this chapter, we will explore the OpenCV functions to store and read our data. In many applications, such as calibration or machine learning, when we are done with the calculations, we need to save the results in order to retrieve them in the next executions. For this purpose, OpenCV provides an XML/YAML persistence layer.

Writing to a file storage

To write a file with some OpenCV data or other numeric data, we can use the FileStorage class using the streaming c operator such as STL streaming:

```
#include "opencv2/opencv.hpp"
using namespace cv;

int main(int, char** argv)
{
    // create our writter
```

```
FileStorage fs("test.yml", FileStorage::WRITE);
// Save an int
int fps= 5;
fs << "fps" << fps;
// Create some mat sample
Mat m1= Mat::eye(2,3, CV_32F);
 Mat m2= Mat::ones(3,2, CV_32F);
 Mat result= (m1+1).mul(m1+3);
 // write the result
fs << "Result" << result;
// release the file
fs.release();

FileStorage fs2("test.yml", FileStorage::READ);

Mat r;
fs2["Result"] >> r;
std::cout << r << std::endl;

fs2.release();

return 0;
}
```

To create a file storage where we save the data, we only need to call the constructor by giving a path filename with the desired extension format (XML or YAML) with the second parameter set to WRITE:

```
FileStorage fs("test.yml", FileStorage::WRITE);
```

If we want to save the data, we only need to use the stream operator by giving an identifier in the first stage and the matrix or value that we want to save in the later stage. For example, to save an int, we need to write the following code:

```
int fps= 5;
fs << "fps" << fps;
```

A mat is as follows:

```
Mat m1= Mat::eye(2,3, CV_32F);
Mat m2= Mat::ones(3,2, CV_32F);
Mat result= (m1+1).mul(m1+3);
// write the result
fs << "Result" << result;
```

The result of the preceding code is in YAML format, which is as follows:

```
%YAML:1.0
fps: 5
Result: !!opencv-matrix
   rows: 2
   cols: 3
   dt: f
   data: [ 8., 3., 3., 3., 8., 3. ]
```

Reading from a saved file previously is very similar to save functions:

```cpp
#include "opencv2/opencv.hpp"
using namespace cv;

int main(int, char** argv)
{
    FileStorage fs2("test.yml", FileStorage::READ);

    Mat r;
    fs2["Result"] >> r;
    std::cout << r << std::endl;

    fs2.release();

    return 0;
}
```

First, we have to open a saved file with the `FileStorage` constructor using the appropriate path and `FileStorage::READ` parameters:

```cpp
FileStorage fs2("test.yml", FileStorage::READ);
```

To read any stored variable, we only need to use the common `>>` stream operator using our `FileStorage` object and the identifier with the `[]` operator:

```cpp
Mat r;
fs2["Result"] >> r;
```

Summary

In this chapter, we learned the basics of how to access images and videos and how they are stored in matrices.

We learned the basic matrix operations and other basic OpenCV classes to store pixels, vectors, and so on.

Finally, we learned how to save our data in files to allow them to be read in other applications or executions.

In the next chapter, we will learn how to create our first application by learning the basics of a Graphical User Interface that OpenCV gives us. We will create buttons and sliders and introduce some image processing basics.

3
Learning the Graphical User Interface and Basic Filtering

In the previous chapter, we learned the basic classes and structures of OpenCV and the most important class called `Mat`.

We learned how to read and save images, videos, and the internal structure in the memory of images.

We are ready to work now, but we need to show our results and have some basic interaction with our images. OpenCV provides us with a few basic user interfaces to work with and help create our applications and prototypes.

To better understand how the user interface works, we are going to create a small application called **PhotoTool** at the end of this chapter. In this application, we will learn how to use filters and color conversions.

In this chapter, we will cover the following topics:

- The basic OpenCV user interface
- The OpenCV QT interface
- Sliders and buttons
- An advanced user interface—OpenGL
- Color conversion
- Basic filters

Introducing the OpenCV user interface

OpenCV has its own cross-operating system user interface that allows developers to create their own applications without the need to learn complex libraries for the user interface.

The OpenCV user interface is basic, but it gives Computer Vision developers the basic functions to create and manage their software developments. All of them are native and optimized for real-time use.

OpenCV provides two options for the user interface:

- A basic interface based on native user interfaces, such as Cocoa or Carbon for OS X and GTK for Linux or Windows user interfaces, that are selected by default when you compile OpenCV.

- A slightly more advanced interface based on the QT library that is cross-platform. You have to enable the QT option manually in CMake before you compile OpenCV.

A basic graphical user interface with OpenCV

We are going to create a basic user interface with OpenCV. The OpenCV user interface allows us to create windows, add images to it, move it, resize it, and destroy it.

The user interface is in the OpenCV's module called highui:

```cpp
#include <iostream>
#include <string>
#include <sstream>
using namespace std;

// OpenCV includes
#include "opencv2/core.hpp"
#include "opencv2/highgui.hpp"
using namespace cv;

const int CV_GUI_NORMAL= 0x10;

int main( int argc, const char** argv )
{
  // Read images
  Mat lena= imread("../lena.jpg");
  Mat photo= imread("../photo.jpg");

  // Create windows
  namedWindow("Lena", CV_GUI_NORMAL);
  namedWindow("Photo", WINDOW_AUTOSIZE);

  // Move window
  moveWindow("Lena", 10, 10);
  moveWindow("Photo", 520, 10);

  // show images
  imshow("Lena", lena);
  imshow("Photo", photo);

  // Resize window, only non autosize
  resizeWindow("Lena", 512, 512);

  // wait for any key press
  waitKey(0);
```

```
// Destroy the windows
destroyWindow("Lena");
destroyWindow("Photo");

// Create 10 windows
for(int i =0; i< 10; i++)
{
  ostringstream ss;
  ss << "Photo " << i;
  namedWindow(ss.str());
  moveWindow(ss.str(), 20*i, 20*i);
  imshow(ss.str(), photo);
}

waitKey(0);
// Destroy all windows
destroyAllWindows();
return 0;
}
```

Let's understand the code.

The first task that we need to perform in order to enable a Graphical User Interface is import the OpenCV's module highui:

```
#include "opencv2/highgui.hpp"
```

Now, we are prepared to create our new windows, and then we need to load some images that are to be shown:

```
// Read images
Mat lena= imread("../lena.jpg");
Mat photo= imread("../photo.jpg");
```

To create the windows, we use the namedWindow function. This function has two parameters: the first parameter is a constant string with the window's name, and the second parameter is the flags that we require, which is optional:

```
namedWindow("Lena", CV_GUI_NORMAL);
namedWindow("Photo", WINDOW_AUTOSIZE);
```

In our case, we create two windows: the first window is called Lena and the second is called Photo.

By default, there are the three flags for QT and native interfaces:

- WINDOW_NORMAL: This flag allows the user to resize the window
- WINDOW_AUTOSIZE: If this flag is set, the window size is automatically adjusted to fit the display image and it is not possible to resize the window
- WINDOW_OPENGL: This flag enables OpenGL support

QT has some more flags, which are as follows:

- WINDOW_FREERATIO or WINDOW_KEEPRATIO: If set to WINDOW_FREERATIO, then the image is adjusted with no respect to its ratio. If set to WINDOW_FREERATIO, then the image is adjusted with respect to its ratio.
- CV_GUI_NORMAL or CV_GUI_EXPANDED: The first flag enables the basic interface without the status bar and toolbar. The second flag enables the most advanced graphical user interface with the status bar and toolbar.

> If we compile OpenCV with QT, all the windows that we create are, by default, in the expanded interface, but we can use native and more basic interfaces by adding the CV_GUI_NORMAL flag.
>
> By default, the flags are WINDOW_AUTOSIZE, WINDOW_KEEPRATIO, and CV_GUI_EXPANDED.

When we create multiple windows, they are superimposed one above the other, but we can move the windows to any area of our desktop with the moveWindow function:

```
// Move window
moveWindow("Lena", 10, 10);
moveWindow("Photo", 520, 10);
```

In our code, we move the Lena window to the left 10 pixels 10 pixels to the top; and the Photo window to the left 520 pixels and 10 pixels to the top:

```
// show images
imshow("Lena", lena);
imshow("Photo", photo);
// Resize window, only non autosize
resizeWindow("Lena", 512, 512);
```

After showing the images that we loaded previously with the imshow function, we resize the Lena window to 512 pixels, calling the resizeWindow function. This function has three parameters: window name, width, and height.

The specific window size is for the image area. Toolbars are not counted. Only windows without the enabled `WINDOW_AUTOSIZE` flag can be resized.

After waiting for a key press with the `waitKey` function, we will remove or delete our windows with the `destroyWindow` function in which the name of the window is the only parameter that is required:

```
waitKey(0);

// Destroy the windows
destroyWindow("Lena");
destroyWindow("Photo");
```

OpenCV has a function that is used to remove all the windows that we create in only one call. The function is called `destroyAllWindows`. To show how this function works, in our sample we create 10 windows and wait for a key press. When the user presses any key, we destroy all the windows. Anyway, OpenCV automatically handles the destruction of all the windows when the application is terminated, and it is not necessary to call this function at the end of our application:

```
// Create 10 windows
for(int i =0; i< 10; i++)
{
    ostringstream ss;
    ss << "Photo " << i;
    namedWindow(ss.str());
    moveWindow(ss.str(), 20*i, 20*i);
    imshow(ss.str(), photo);
}

waitKey(0);
// Destroy all windows
destroyAllWindows();
```

The result of this code can be seen in the following images in two steps. The first image shows two windows:

After pressing any key, the application continues and draws several windows by changing their positions:

The graphical user interface with QT

The QT user interface gives us more control and options to work with our images.

The interface is divided into three main areas:

- The toolbar
- The image area
- The status bar

The toolbar has the following buttons from left to right:

- Four buttons for panning
- Zoom x1
- Zoom x30 and show labels
- Zoom in

- Zoom out
- Save the current image
- Show the properties windows

These options can be seen more clearly in the following screenshot:

The image area shows an image and a contextual menu when we push the right mouse button over the image. This area can show an overlay message at the top of the area using the `displayOverlay` function. This function accepts three parameters: the window name, the text that we want to show, and the period in milliseconds when the overlay text is displayed. If the time is set to `0`, the text never disappears:

```
// Display Overlay
displayOverlay("Lena", "Overlay 5secs", 5000);
```

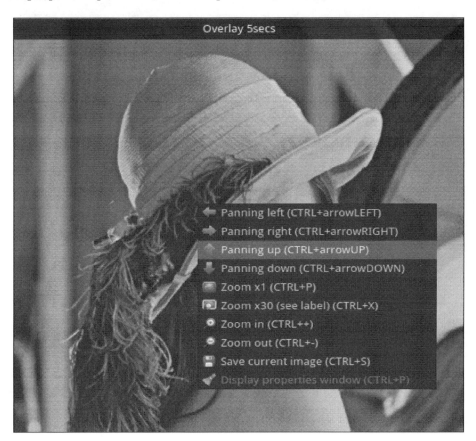

Finally, the status bar shows the bottom part of the window, the pixel value, and the position of the coordinates in the image:

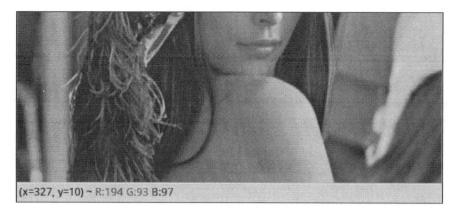

We can use the status bar to show messages, such as an overlay. The function that can change the status bar message is `displayStatusBar`. This function has the same parameters as overlay functions: the window name, the text to show, and the period of time to show it:

Adding slider and mouse events to our interfaces

Mouse events and slider controls are very useful in Computer Vision and OpenCV. Using these controls, users can interact directly with the interface and change the properties of their input images or variables.

In this section, we are going to introduce you to the concepts of adding slider and mouse events for basic interactions. To understand this correctly, we will create a small project, where we paint green circles in the image using the mouse events and blur the image with the slider:

```cpp
// Create a variable to save the position value in track
int blurAmount=15;

// Trackbar call back function
static void onChange(int pos, void* userInput);

//Mouse callback
static void onMouse( int event, int x, int y, int, void* userInput );

int main( int argc, const char** argv )
{
  // Read images
  Mat lena= imread("../lena.jpg");

  // Create windows
  namedWindow("Lena");

  // create a trackbark
  createTrackbar("Lena", "Lena", &blurAmount, 30, onChange, &lena);

  setMouseCallback("Lena", onMouse, &lena);

  // Call to onChange to init
  onChange(blurAmount, &lena);

  // wait app for a key to exit
  waitKey(0);

  // Destroy the windows
  destroyWindow("Lena");

  return 0;
}
```

Let's understand the code!

First, we create a variable to save the slider position, and then we need to save the slider position for access from other functions:

```
// Create a variable to save the position value in track
int blurAmount=15;
```

Now, we define our callbacks for our slider and mouse events that are required for the OpenCV setMouseCallbac and createTrackbar functions:

```
// Trackbar call back function
static void onChange(int pos, void* userInput);

//Mouse callback
static void onMouse( int event, int x, int y, int, void* userInput );
```

In the main function, we load an image and create a new window called Lena:

```
int main( int argc, const char** argv )
{
  // Read images
  Mat lena= imread("../lena.jpg");

  // Create windows
  namedWindow("Lena");
```

It is time to create the slider. OpenCV has the createTrackbar function that is used to generate a slider with the following parameters in order:

- The track bar name.
- The window name.
- An integer pointer to be used as a value; this parameter is optional. If the pointer value is set, the slider gets this position during its creation.
- The maximal position on the slider.
- The callback function when the position slider changes.
- The user data to be sent to the callback. It can be used to send data to callbacks without using global variables:

  ```
  // create a trackbark
  createTrackbar("Lena", "Lena", &blurAmount, 30, onChange,
  &lena);
  ```

After creating the slider, we add the mouse events that allow you to paint circles when the user pushes the left mouse button. OpenCV has the `setMouseCallback` function. This function has three parameters, which are as follows:

- The window name where we get the mouse events
- The `callback` function to be called when there are mouse interactions
- User data refers to any data that will be sent to the callback function when it's fired. In our example, we'll send the entire Lena image:

```
setMouseCallback("Lena", onMouse, &lena);
```

To finalize the `main` function, we only need to initialize the image with the same parameter as the slider. To perform the initialization, we only need to call the `callback` function manually and wait for events before we close the windows:

```
// Call to onChange to init
onChange(blurAmount, &lena);

// wait app for a key to exit
waitKey(0);

// Destroy the windows
destroyWindow("Lena");
```

The slider callback applies a basic blur filter to the image using the slider value as a blur quantity:

```
// Trackbar call back function
static void onChange(int pos, void* userData)
{
  if(pos <= 0)
    return;
  // Aux variable for result
  Mat imgBlur;

  // Get the pointer input image
  Mat* img= (Mat*)userInput;

  // Apply a blur filter
  blur(*img, imgBlur, Size(pos, pos));

  // Show the result
  imshow("Lena", imgBlur);
}
```

This function checks whether the slider value is 0 using the `pos` variable; in this case, we do not apply the filter because it generates a bad execution. We cannot apply a 0 pixels blur.

After checking the slider value, we create an empty matrix called `imgBlur` to store the blur result.

To retrieve the image sent via the user data in the `callback` function, we have to cast the `void* userData` to correct the `pointer Mat*` image type.

Now, we have the correct variables to be applied to the blur filter. The blur function applies a basic median filter to an input image, `*img` in our case, to an output image. The last parameter is the size of a blur kernel (a kernel is a small matrix used to calculate the means of convolution between the kernel and image) that we want to apply. In our case, we are using a squared kernel of the `pos` size.

Finally, we only need to update the image interface using the `imshow` function.

The mouse events callback has five input parameters: the first parameter defines the event type, the second and third parameters define the mouse position, the fourth parameter defines the wheel movement, and the fifth parameter defines the user input data.

The mouse event types are shown in the following table:

Event type	Description
EVENT_MOUSEMOVE	When the user moves the mouse
EVENT_LBUTTONDOWN	When the user pushes the left mouse button
EVENT_RBUTTONDOWN	When the user pushes the right mouse button
EVENT_MBUTTONDOWN	When the user pushes the middle mouse button
EVENT_LBUTTONUP	When the user releases the left mouse button
EVENT_RBUTTONUP	When the user releases the right mouse button
EVENT_MBUTTONUP	When the user releases the middle mouse button
EVENT_LBUTTONDBLCLK	When the user double-clicks with the left mouse button
EVENT_RBUTTONDBLCLK	When the user double-clicks with the right mouse button
EVENT_MBUTTONDBLCLK	When the user double-clicks with the middle mouse button
EVENTMOUSEWHEEL	When the user does a vertical scroll with the mouse wheel
EVENT_MOUSEHWHEEL	When the user does a horizontal scroll with the mouse wheel

In our sample, we only go to manage events that come from a left-push mouse button, and then any other event different from EVENT_LBUTTONDOWN is discarded. After discarding other events, we get the input image, such as a slider callback, and draw a circle in the image with the circle OpenCV function:

```
//Mouse callback
static void onMouse( int event, int x, int y, int, void* userInput )
{
  if( event != EVENT_LBUTTONDOWN )
          return;

  // Get the pointer input image
  Mat* img= (Mat*)userInput;

  // Draw circle
  circle(*img, Point(x, y), 10, Scalar(0,255,0), 3);

  // Call on change to get blurred image
  onChange(blurAmount, img);

}
```

Adding buttons to a user interface

In the previous chapter, we learned how to create normal or QT interfaces and interact with them with a mouse and slider, but we can create different types of buttons as well.

 Buttons are only supported in QT Windows.

The types of buttons supported are as follows:

- The push button
- The checkbox
- The radiobox

The buttons only appear in the control panel. The control panel is an independent window per program, where we can attach buttons and track bars.

To show the control panel, we can push the last toolbar button, right-click on any part of the QT window, and select the **Display properties** window or the *Ctrl + P* shortcut.

Let's see how to create a basic sample with buttons. The code is large, and we will first explain the main function and later explain each callback separately to understand each one of them:

```
Mat img;
bool applyGray=false;
bool applyBlur=false;
bool applySobel=false;
...
int main( int argc, const char** argv )
{
  // Read images
  img= imread("../lena.jpg");

  // Create windows
  namedWindow("Lena");

  // create Buttons
  createButton("Blur", blurCallback, NULL, QT_CHECKBOX, 0);

  createButton("Gray",grayCallback,NULL,QT_RADIOBOX, 0);
  createButton("RGB",bgrCallback,NULL,QT_RADIOBOX, 1);

  createButton("Sobel",sobelCallback,NULL,QT_PUSH_BUTTON, 0);

  // wait app for a key to exit
  waitKey(0);

  // Destroy the windows
  destroyWindow("Lena");

  return 0;
}
```

We are going to apply three types of blur fiters, a sobel fiter, and a color conversion to gray. All these filters are optional and the user can choose each one of them using the buttons that we are going to create. Then, in order to get the status of each filter, we create three global Boolean variables:

```
bool applyGray=false;
bool applyBlur=false;
bool applySobel=false;
```

In the main function after we load the image and create the window, we have to use the `createButton` function to create each button.

There are three button types defined in OpenCV, which are as follows:

- QT_CHECKBOX
- QT_RADIOBOX
- QT_PUSH_BUTTON

Each button has five parameters with the following order:

- The button name
- The callback function
- A pointer to user variable data passed to callback
- The button type
- The default initialized state used for the checkbox and radiobox button types
- Then, we create a blur checkbox button, two radio buttons for color conversion, and a push button for the Sobel filter:

  ```
  // create Buttons
  createButton("Blur", blurCallback, NULL, QT_CHECKBOX, 0);

  createButton("Gray",grayCallback,NULL,QT_RADIOBOX, 0);
  createButton("RGB",bgrCallback,NULL,QT_RADIOBOX, 1);

  createButton("Sobel",sobelCallback,NULL,QT_PUSH_BUTTON,
      0);
  ```

- This is the most important part of the main function. We are going to explore the callback functions. Each callback changes its status variable to call another function called `applyFilters` and adds the filters activated by the input image:

  ```
  void grayCallback(int state, void* userData)
  {
    applyGray= true;
    applyFilters();
  }
  void bgrCallback(int state, void* userData)
  {
    applyGray= false;
    applyFilters();
  }
  ```

```
void blurCallback(int state, void* userData)
{
  applyBlur= (bool)state;
  applyFilters();
}

void sobelCallback(int state, void* userData)
{
  applySobel= !applySobel;
  applyFilters();
}
```

- The `applyFilters` function checks the status variable for each filter:

```
void applyFilters(){
  Mat result;
  img.copyTo(result);
  if(applyGray){
    cvtColor(result, result, COLOR_BGR2GRAY);
  }
  if(applyBlur){
    blur(result, result, Size(5,5));
  }
  if(applySobel){
    Sobel(result, result, CV_8U, 1, 1);
  }
  imshow("Lena", result);
}
```

To change the color to gray, we use the `cvtColor` function that accepts three parameters: an input image, an output image, and the color conversion type.

The most useful color spaces conversions are as follows:

- RGB or BGR to gray (`COLOR_RGB2GRAY`, `COLOR_BGR2GRAY`)
- RGB or BGR to YcrCb (or YCC) (`COLOR_RGB2YCrCb`, `COLOR_BGR2YCrCb`)
- RGB or BGR to HSV (`COLOR_RGB2HSV`, `COLOR_BGR2HSV`)
- RGB or BGR to Luv (`COLOR_RGB2Luv`, `COLOR_BGR2Luv`)
- Gray to RGB or BGR (`COLOR_GRAY2RGB`, `COLOR_GRAY2BGR`)

We can see that the code is easy to memorize.

Remember that OpenCV works, by default, with the BGR format, and the color conversion is different for RGB and BGR, when converting to gray. Some developers think that gray equals *R+G+B/3*, but the optimal gray value is called **luminosity** and has the formula *0.21*R + 0.72*G + 0.07*B*.

The blur filter was described in the previous section. Finally, if the `applySobel` variable is `true`, we apply the sobel filter.

The sobel filter is an image derivatives that uses the sobel operator, commonly used to detect edges. OpenCV allow us to generate different derivatives with different kernel sizes, but the most common is a 3x3 kernel used to calculate the x derivatives or y derivatives.

The most important sobel parameters are as follows:

- An input image
- An output image
- An output image depth (`CV_8U`, `CV_16U`, `CV_32F`, `CV_64F`)
- The order of the derivatives x
- The order of the derivatives y
- The kernel size (3 value by default)
- To generate a 3x3 kernel and first x order derivatives, we have to use the following parameters:

  ```
  Sobel(input, output, CV_8U, 1, 0);
  ```

- To generate the y order derivatives, we use the following parameters:

  ```
  Sobel(input, output, CV_8U, 0, 1);
  ```

In our example, we use the x and y derivatives simultaneously to overwrite the input:

```
Sobel(result, result, CV_8U, 1, 1);
```

The output of the x and y derivatives is as shown:

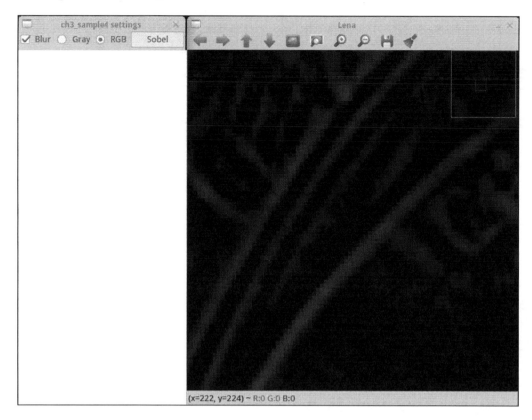

OpenGL support

OpenCV includes OpenGL support. OpenGL is a graphical library that is integrated in graphic cards as a standard. OpenGL allow us to draw from 2D to complex 3D scenes.

OpenCV includes OpenGL support due to the importance of representing 3D spaces in some tasks. To allow a window support in OpenGL, we have to set up the WINDOW_OPENGL flag when we create the window with the namedWindow call.

The following code creates a window with OpenGL support and draws a rotated plane that shows the web camera frames:

```
Mat frame;
GLfloat angle= 0.0;
GLuint texture;
```

```
VideoCapture camera;

int loadTexture() {

    if (frame.data==NULL) return -1;
glGenTextures(1, &texture);
    glBindTexture( GL_TEXTURE_2D, texture );
    glTexParameteri(GL_TEXTURE_2D,GL_TEXTURE_MAG_FILTER,GL_LINEAR);
    glTexParameteri(GL_TEXTURE_2D,GL_TEXTURE_MIN_FILTER,GL_LINEAR);
    glPixelStorei(GL_UNPACK_ALIGNMENT, 1);

    glTexImage2D(GL_TEXTURE_2D, 0, GL_RGB, frame.cols, frame.rows,0,
GL_BGR, GL_UNSIGNED_BYTE, frame.data);
    return 0;

}

void on_opengl(void* param)
{
    glLoadIdentity();
    // Load frame Texture
    glBindTexture( GL_TEXTURE_2D, texture );
    // Rotate plane before draw
    glRotatef( angle, 1.0f, 1.0f, 1.0f );
    // Create the plane and set the texture coordinates
    glBegin (GL_QUADS);
        // first point and coordinate texture
     glTexCoord2d(0.0,0.0);
     glVertex2d(-1.0,-1.0);
        // seccond point and coordinate texture
     glTexCoord2d(1.0,0.0);
     glVertex2d(+1.0,-1.0);
        // third point and coordinate texture
     glTexCoord2d(1.0,1.0);
     glVertex2d(+1.0,+1.0);
        // last point and coordinate texture
     glTexCoord2d(0.0,1.0);
     glVertex2d(-1.0,+1.0);
    glEnd();

}
```

```
int main( int argc, const char** argv )
{
    // Open WebCam
    camera.open(0);
    if(!camera.isOpened())
        return -1;

    // Create new windows
    namedWindow("OpenGL Camera", WINDOW_OPENGL);

    // Enable texture
    glEnable( GL_TEXTURE_2D );

    setOpenGlDrawCallback("OpenGL Camera", on_opengl);

    while(waitKey(30)!='q'){
        camera >> frame;
        // Create first texture
        loadTexture();
        updateWindow("OpenGL Camera");
        angle =angle+4;
    }


    // Destroy the windows
    destroyWindow("OpenGL Camera");

    return 0;
}
```

Let's understand the code.

The first task is to create the required global variables where we store the video capture, save the frames, control the animation angle plane, and the OpenGL texture:

```
Mat frame;
GLfloat angle= 0.0;
GLuint texture;
VideoCapture camera;
```

In our main function, we have to create the video camera capture to retrieve the camera frames:

```
camera.open(0);
    if(!camera.isOpened())
        return -1;
```

If the camera is opened correctly, then we have to create our window with OpenGL support using the `WINDOW_OPENGL` flag:

```
// Create new windows
namedWindow("OpenGL Camera", WINDOW_OPENGL);
```

In our example, we want to draw the images in a plane that come from the web camera, and then we need to enable the OpenGL textures:

```
// Enable texture
glEnable( GL_TEXTURE_2D );
```

Now, we are ready to draw with OpenGL in our window, but we need set up a draw OpenGL callback such as a typical OpenGL application. OpenCV give us the `setOpenGLDrawCallback` function that has two parameters: the window name and the callback function:

```
setOpenGlDrawCallback("OpenGL Camera", on_opengl);
```

With the OpenCV window and callback function defined, we need to create a loop to load the texture and update the window content by calling the OpenGL draw callback; finally, we need to update the angle position.

To update the window content, we use the OpenCV function update window with the window name as the parameter:

```
while(waitKey(30)!='q'){
        camera >> frame;
        // Create first texture
        loadTexture();
        updateWindow("OpenGL Camera");
        angle =angle+4;
    }
```

We are in the loop while the user press the *q* key.

Before we compile our application sample, we need to define the `loadTexture` function and our `on_opengl` callback draw function.

The `loadTexture` function converts our `Mat` frame to an OpenGL texture image that is ready to be loaded and used in each callback drawing. Before we load the image as a texture, we need to ensure that we have data in our frame matrix to check whether the data variable object is not empty:

```
if (frame.data==NULL) return -1;
```

If we have data in our matrix frame, then we can create the OpenGL texture binding and set the OpenGL texture parameters as a linear interpolation:

```
glGenTextures(1, &texture);

glBindTexture( GL_TEXTURE_2D, texture );
    glTexParameteri(GL_TEXTURE_2D,GL_TEXTURE_MAG_FILTER,GL_LINEAR);
    glTexParameteri(GL_TEXTURE_2D,GL_TEXTURE_MIN_FILTER,GL_LINEAR);
```

Now, we need to define how the pixels are stored in our matrix and how to generate the pixels with the OpenGL's `glTexImage2D` function. It's very important to note that OpenGL uses the RGB format and OpenCV has the BGR format by default, and we need to set it up correctly in this function:

```
glPixelStorei(GL_UNPACK_ALIGNMENT, 1);
glTexImage2D(GL_TEXTURE_2D, 0, GL_RGB, frame.cols, frame.rows,0, GL_
BGR, GL_UNSIGNED_BYTE, frame.data);
    return 0;
```

Now, we only need to finish drawing our plane for every callback when we call the `updateWindow` in the main loop. We use the common OpenGL functions, and then we load the identity OpenGL matrix to reset all our previous changes:

```
glLoadIdentity();
```

Load the frame texture into the memory:

```
// Load Texture
glBindTexture( GL_TEXTURE_2D, texture );
```

Before we draw our plane, we apply all the transformations to our scene; in our case, we are going to rotate our plane in the (1, 1, 1) axis:

```
// Rotate plane
glRotatef( angle, 1.0f, 1.0f, 1.0f );
```

Now, we have the scene set correctly to draw our plane, so we will draw quads faces and use `glBegin(GL_QUADS)` for this purpose:

```
// Create the plane and set the texture coordinates
glBegin (GL_QUADS);
```

We draw a plane centered at the (0, 0) position with a two units of size. Then, we have to define the texture coordinate to be used and the vertex position using the glTextCoord2D and glVertex2D functions:

```
    // first point and coordinate texture
glTexCoord2d(0.0,0.0);
glVertex2d(-1.0,-1.0);
    // seccond point and coordinate texture
glTexCoord2d(1.0,0.0);
glVertex2d(+1.0,-1.0);
    // third point and coordinate texture
glTexCoord2d(1.0,1.0);
glVertex2d(+1.0,+1.0);
    // last point and coordinate texture
glTexCoord2d(0.0,1.0);
glVertex2d(-1.0,+1.0);
    glEnd();
```

 This OpenGL code is becoming obsolete, but it is important to better understand the OpenCV and OpenGL integration without the complex OpenGL code. To introduce you to modern OpenGL, read *Introduction to Modern OpenGL, Pack Publishing*.

We can see the result in the following image:

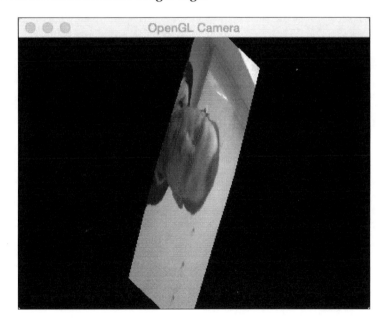

Summary

In this chapter, we learned how to create different types of user interface to show images or 3D interfaces using OpenGL. We learned how to create sliders and buttons and draw in 3D. We learned some basic image processing filters as well.

In the next chapter, we will learn how to construct a complete photo tool application using all that we learned using the graphical user interface. We will also learn how to apply multiple filters to an input image.

4

Delving into Histograms and Filters

In the previous chapter, we learned the basics of user interfaces in OpenCV using QT or native libraries and how to use advanced OpenGL user interfaces. We learned basic color conversions and filters that helped us create our first application.

In this chapter, we will cover the following topics:

- Histogram and histogram equalization
- Look up tables
- The blur and median blur
- The Gaussian Canny filter
- Image color equalization
- Understanding conversion between image types

After we learn the basics of OpenCV and user interfaces, we will create our first complete application and a basic photo tool with the following functionalities in this chapter:

- Calculate and draw a histogram
- Histogram equalization
- The lomography camera effect
- The cartoonize effect

This application will help you understand how to create a whole project from scratch and understand the histogram concept. We will see how to equalize the histogram of a color image and create two effects using a combination of filters and the use of look up tables.

Generating a CMake script file

Before we start creating our source file, we will generate the `CMakeLists.txt` file that will allow us to compile our project, structure, and executable. The following `cmake` script is simple and basic but enough to compile and generate the executable:

```
cmake_minimum_required (VERSION 2.6)

cmake_policy(SET CMP0012 NEW)

PROJECT(Chapter4_Phototool)

# Requires OpenCV
FIND_PACKAGE( OpenCV 3.0.0 REQUIRED )

include_directories(${OpenCV_INCLUDE_DIRS})
link_directories(${OpenCV_LIB_DIR})

ADD_EXECUTABLE( ${PROJECT_NAME} main.cpp )
TARGET_LINK_LIBRARIES( ${PROJECT_NAME} ${OpenCV_LIBS} )
```

Let's try to understand the script file.

The first line indicates the minimum `cmake` version required to generate our project, and the second line sets the `CMP0012` policy variable to allow you to identify numbers and Boolean constants and remove the CMake warning if it is not set:

```
cmake_minimum_required (VERSION 2.6)
cmake_policy(SET CMP0012 NEW)
```

After these two lines, we define the project name:

```
PROJECT(Chapter4_Phototool)
```

Of course, we need to include the OpenCV library. The first thing to do is find the library and show a message about the OpenCV library version with the MESSAGE function:

```
# Requires OpenCV
FIND_PACKAGE( OpenCV 3.0.0 REQUIRED )
MESSAGE("OpenCV version : ${OpenCV_VERSION}")
```

If the library with the minimum version 3.0 is found, then we include the headers and library files in our project:

```
include_directories(${OpenCV_INCLUDE_DIRS})
link_directories(${OpenCV_LIB_DIR})
```

Now, we only need to add the source files that are to be compiled; in order to link them to the OpenCV library, we use the project name variable as an executable name and use only a single source file called `main.cpp`:

```
ADD_EXECUTABLE( ${PROJECT_NAME} main.cpp )
TARGET_LINK_LIBRARIES( ${PROJECT_NAME} ${OpenCV_LIBS} )
```

Creating the Graphical User Interface

Before we start with the image processing algorithms, we will create the main user interface for our application. We will use a QT-based user interface to allow us to create single buttons.

The application receives one input parameter to load the image to be processed, and we will create the following four buttons:

- **Show histogram**
- **Equalize histogram**
- **Lomography effect**
- **Cartoonize effect**

We can see the four results in the following screenshot:

Let's develop our project. First of all, we will include the required OpenCV headers. We define an `img` matrix to store the input image, and create a constant string to use the new command-line parser, which is only available in OpenCV 3.0. In this constant, we allow only two input parameters: common help and the required image input:

```
// OpenCV includes
#include "opencv2/core/utility.hpp"
#include "opencv2/imgproc.hpp"
#include "opencv2/highgui.hpp"
using namespace cv;
// OpenCV command line parser functions
// Keys accecpted by command line parser
const char* keys =
{
    "{help h usage ? | | print this message}"
    "{@image | | Image to process}"
};
```

The `main` function starts with the command-line parser variable. We then set the instructions and print the help message. The following lines will help you set up the help instructions for our final executable:

```
int main( int argc, const char** argv )
{
    CommandLineParser parser(argc, argv, keys);
    parser.about("Chapter 4. PhotoTool v1.0.0");
    //If requires help show
    if (parser.has("help"))
    {
        parser.printMessage();
        return 0;
    }
```

If the user doesn't require help, then we need to get the file path image in an `imgFile` variable string and check whether all the required parameters are added to the `parser.check()` function:

```
String imgFile= parser.get<String>(0);

    // Check if params are correctly parsed in his variables
    if (!parser.check())
    {
        parser.printErrors();
        return 0;
    }
```

Now, we can read the image file with the `imread` function and then create the window in which the input image will be shown later using the `namedWindow` function:

```
// Load image to process
img= imread(imgFile);
// Create window
namedWindow("Input");
```

With the image loaded and window created, we only need to create the buttons for our interface and link them to the `callback` functions. Each `callback` function is defined in the source code, and we will explain them later in this chapter. We will create the buttons with the `createButton` function with the `QT_PUSH_BUTTON` constant in the button style:

```
// Create UI buttons
createButton("Show histogram", showHistoCallback, NULL, QT_PUSH_
BUTTON, 0);
createButton("Equalize histogram", equalizeCallback, NULL, QT_
PUSH_BUTTON, 0);
createButton("Lomography effect", lomoCallback, NULL, QT_PUSH_
BUTTON, 0);
createButton("Cartonize effect", cartoonCallback, NULL, QT_PUSH_
BUTTON, 0);
```

To complete our `main` function, we show the input image and wait for a key press to finish our application:

```
// Show image
imshow("Input", img);
waitKey(0);
return 0;
```

Now, we only need to define the `callback` functions in the following sections, and we will define and describe each one of them.

Drawing a histogram

A histogram is a statistical graphic representation of variable distribution. This allows us to understand the density estimation and probability distribution of data. The histogram is created by dividing the entire range of variable values into a fixed number of intervals and then counting how many values fall into each interval.

If we apply this histogram concept to an image, it seems to be complex to understand, but it is really very simple. In a gray image, our variable values can take any possible gray value ranging from 0 to 255, and the density is the number of pixels in the image that have this value. This means that we have to count the number of image pixels that have the value 0, count the number of pixels of value 1, and so on.

The callback function that shows the histogram of the input image is called showHistoCallback. This function calculates the histogram of each channel image and shows the result of each histogram channel in a new image.

Now, let's check the following code:

```
void showHistoCallback(int state, void* userData)
{
    // Separate image in BRG
    vector<Mat> bgr;
    split( img, bgr );

    // Create the histogram for 256 bins
    // The number of possibles values [0..255]
    int numbins= 256;

    /// Set the ranges ( for B,G,R) ), last is not included
    float range[] = { 0, 256 } ;
    const float* histRange = { range };

    Mat b_hist, g_hist, r_hist;

    calcHist( &bgr[0], 1, 0, Mat(), b_hist, 1, &numbins,
        &histRange );
    calcHist( &bgr[1], 1, 0, Mat(), g_hist, 1, &numbins,
        &histRange );
    calcHist( &bgr[2], 1, 0, Mat(), r_hist, 1, &numbins,
        &histRange );

    // Draw the histogram
    // We go to draw lines for each channel
    int width= 512;
    int height= 300;
    // Create image with gray base
    Mat histImage( height, width, CV_8UC3, Scalar(20,20,20) );
```

```
// Normalize the histograms to height of image
normalize(b_hist, b_hist, 0, height, NORM_MINMAX );
normalize(g_hist, g_hist, 0, height, NORM_MINMAX );
normalize(r_hist, r_hist, 0, height, NORM_MINMAX );

int binStep= cvRound((float)width/(float)numbins);
for( int i=1; i< numbins; i++)
{
  line( histImage,
    Point( binStep*(i-1), height-cvRound(b_hist.at<float>(i-1) ) ),
      Point( binStep*(i), height-cvRound(b_hist.at<float>(i) ) ),
        Scalar(255,0,0));
  line( histImage,
    Point( binStep*(i-1), height-cvRound(g_hist.at<float>(i-1) ) ),
      Point( binStep*(i), height-cvRound(g_hist.at<float>(i) ) ),
        Scalar(0,255,0));
  line( histImage,
    Point( binStep*(i-1), height-cvRound(r_hist.at<float>(i-1) ) ),
      Point( binStep*(i), height-cvRound(r_hist.at<float>(i) ) ),
        Scalar(0,0,255));
}
imshow("Histogram", histImage);
}
```

Let's try to understand how to extract each channel histogram and how to draw it.

First, we need to create three matrices to process each input image channel. We use a `vector` type variable to store each one, and use the split OpenCV function to divide the input image into three channels:

```
// Separate image in BRG
    vector<Mat> bgr;
    split( img, bgr );
```

Now, we will define the number of bins in our histogram; in our case, one bin per possible pixel value:

```
int numbins= 256;
```

Now, we need to define our range of variables and create three matrices to store each histogram:

```
/// Set the ranges ( for B,G,R) )
float range[] = { 0, 256 } ;
const float* histRange = { range };
Mat b_hist, g_hist, r_hist;
```

Now, we can calculate the histogram using the OpenCV `calcHist` function. This function has several parameters, which are as follows:

- The input image; in our case, we use one image channel stored in the `bgr` vector
- The number of images required to calculate the histogram in the input; in our case, we only use one image
- The dimensions of the number channel used to compute the histogram; we use 0 in our case
- The optional mask matrix
- The variable used to store the calculated histogram
- The histogram dimensionality (the dimension of the space where the image (here, it's a gray plane) takes its values); in our case, it's 1
- The number of bins to be calculated; in our case, we use 256 bins, one per pixel value
- The range of the input variable; in our case, it's a range of possible pixel values from 0 to 255

Our `calcHist` function for each channel looks like the following code:

```
calcHist( &bgr[0], 1, 0, Mat(), b_hist, 1, &numbins, &histRange );
    calcHist( &bgr[1], 1, 0, Mat(), g_hist, 1, &numbins,
        &histRange );
    calcHist( &bgr[2], 1, 0, Mat(), r_hist, 1, &numbins,
      &histRange );
```

Now, we have calculated the histogram for each channel. We need to draw each channel histogram and show it to the user. To do this, we will create a color image with a size of 512 x 300 pixels:

```
// Draw the histogram
    // We go to draw lines for each channel
    int width= 512;
    int height= 300;
    // Create image with gray base
    Mat histImage( height, width, CV_8UC3, Scalar(20,20,20) );
```

Before we draw the histogram values in our image, we will normalize the histogram matrices between the `min` value `0` and a `max` value; in our case, the same value as that of the height of our image, 300 pixels:

```
// Normalize the histograms to height of image
normalize(b_hist, b_hist, 0, height, NORM_MINMAX );
normalize(g_hist, g_hist, 0, height, NORM_MINMAX );
normalize(r_hist, r_hist, 0, height, NORM_MINMAX );
```

Now, we need to draw a line from bin 0 to bin 1 and so on. We need to calculate the number of pixels between each bin, and then a `binStep` variable is calculated by dividing the width by the number of bins.

Each small line is drawn from the horizontal position, `i-1` to `i`, and the vertical position is the histogram value in the corresponding `i`. It is drawn with the color channel representation, which is as follows:

```
int binStep= cvRound((float)width/(float)numbins);
  for( int i=1; i< numbins; i++)
  {
    line( histImage,
      Point( binStep*(i-1), height-cvRound(b_hist.at<float>(i-1) ) ),
        Point( binStep*(i), height-cvRound(b_hist.at<float>(i) ) ),
          Scalar(255,0,0));
    line( histImage,
      Point( binStep*(i-1), height-cvRound(g_hist.at<float>(i-1) ) ),
        Point( binStep*(i), height-cvRound(g_hist.at<float>(i) ) ),
          Scalar(0,255,0));
    line( histImage,
      Point( binStep*(i-1), height-cvRound(r_hist.at<float>(i-1) ) ),
        Point( binStep*(i), height-cvRound(r_hist.at<float>(i) ) ),
          Scalar(0,0,255));
  }
```

Finally, we show the histogram image with the `imshow` function:

```
imshow("Histogram", histImage);
```

This is the result of the lena.png image:

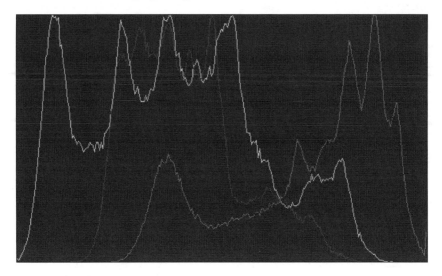

Image color equalization

In this section, we will learn how to equalize a color image. Image equalization and histogram equalization try to obtain a histogram with a uniform distribution of values. The result of equalization is an increase in the contrast of an image. The equalization allows lower local contrast areas to gain higher contrast, spreading out the most frequent intensities.

This method is very useful when the image is almost dark or completely bright and there are very small differences between the background and foreground. Using histogram equalization, we increase the contrast and the details that are over- or under-exposed. This technique is very useful in medical images, such as X-rays.

However, there are two main disadvantages to this method: it increases the background noise and decreases useful signals.

We can see the effect of equalization in the following image and see how the histogram changes and spreads on increasing the image contrast:

Let's try to implement our histogram equalization. We will implement it in the callback function defined in the user interface's code:

```
void equalizeCallback(int state, void* userData)
{
    Mat result;
    // Convert BGR image to YCbCr
    Mat ycrcb;
    cvtColor( img, ycrcb, COLOR_BGR2YCrCb);

    // Split image into channels
    vector<Mat> channels;
    split( ycrcb, channels );

    // Equalize the Y channel only
    equalizeHist( channels[0], channels[0] );

    // Merge the result channels
    merge( channels, ycrcb );

    // Convert color ycrcb to BGR
    cvtColor( ycrcb, result, COLOR_YCrCb2BGR );

    // Show image
    imshow("Equalized", result);
}
```

To equalize a color image, we only need to equalize the luminance channel. We can do this with each color channel, but the result is not usable. Then, we can use any other color image format, such as HSV or YCrCb, that separates the luminance component in an individual channel. We choose this last color format and use a Y channel (luminance) to equalize it. Then, we perform the following steps:

1. We convert our input BGR image into YCrCb using the `cvtColor` function:

```
Mat result;
    // Convert BGR image to YCbCr
    Mat ycrcb;
    cvtColor( img, ycrcb, COLOR_BGR2YCrCb);
```

2. After converting our image, we split the YCrCb image into different `channels` matrices:

```
// Split image into channels
    vector<Mat> channels;
    split( ycrcb, channels );
```

3. We then equalize the histogram only in the `Y channel` using the `equalizeHist` function, which has only two parameters: input and output matrices:

```
// Equalize the Y channel only
    equalizeHist( channels[0], channels[0] );
```

4. Now, we only need to merge the resulted channels and convert the result to the BGR format to show the user the result:

```
// Merge the result channels
    merge( channels, ycrcb );

    // Convert color ycrcb to BGR
    cvtColor( ycrcb, result, COLOR_YCrCb2BGR );

    // Show image
    imshow("Equalized", result);
```

The process applied to a low contrast Lena image will have the following result:

Lomography effect

In this section, we will create another image effect, a photographic effect that is commonly used in different mobile applications, such as Google Camera or Instagram.

In this section, we will discover how to use a **Look up Table** or **LUT**. We will discuss LUTs later in this chapter.

We will learn how to add an over image; in this case, a dark halo to create our desired effect.

The function that implements this effect is the callback `lomoCallback` and has the following code:

```
void lomoCallback(int state, void* userData)
{
    Mat result;

    const double exponential_e = std::exp(1.0);
    // Create Lookup table for color curve effect
    Mat lut(1, 256, CV_8UC1);
    for (int i=0; i<256; i++)
    {
        float x= (float)i/256.0;
        lut.at<uchar>(i)= cvRound( 256 * (1/(1 + pow(exponential_e,
-((x-0.5)/0.1)) )) ) );
    }

    // Split the image channels and apply curve transform only to red
channel
    vector<Mat> bgr;
    split(img, bgr);
    LUT(bgr[2], lut, bgr[2]);
    // merge result
    merge(bgr, result);

    // Create image for halo dark
    Mat halo( img.rows, img.cols, CV_32FC3, Scalar(0.3,0.3,0.3) );
    // Create circle
    circle(halo, Point(img.cols/2, img.rows/2), img.cols/3,
Scalar(1,1,1), -1);
    blur(halo, halo, Size(img.cols/3, img.cols/3));

    // Convert the result to float to allow multiply by 1 factor
    Mat resultf;
    result.convertTo(resultf, CV_32FC3);

    // Multiply our result with halo
    multiply(resultf, halo, resultf);

    // convert to 8 bits
    resultf.convertTo(result, CV_8UC3);

    // show result
    imshow("Lomograpy", result);
}
```

Let's understand the code.

The lomography effect is divided into different steps, but in our example we applied a very simple lomography effect using the following two steps:

1. A color manipulation with a look up table that applies a curve to the red channel

2. A vintage effect that applies a dark halo to the image.

The first step is to manipulate the red color with a curve transform that applies this function:

$$\frac{1}{1 + e^{-\frac{x-0.5}{s}}}$$

This formula generates a curve that makes the dark values darker and light values lighter, where *x* is the possible pixel value (0 to 255) and *s* is a constant that we set to *0.1* in our tutorial. A lower constant value that generates pixels with values lower than 128 is very dark and over 128 is very bright. Values that are near to *1* convert the curve to a line and do not generate our desired effect:

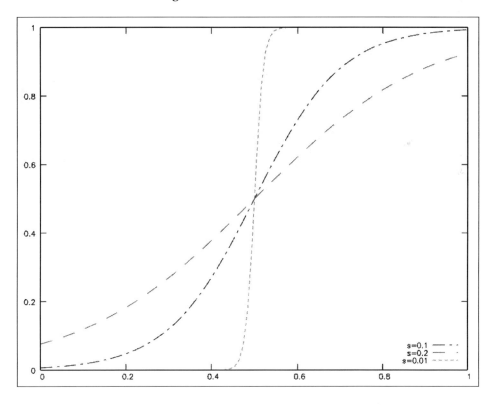

This function is very easy to implement by applying a **Look Up Table**, more commonly called a LUT. A LUT is a vector or table that returns a preprocess value for a given value to perform computation in the memory. A LUT is a common technique used to spare CPU cycles by avoiding performing costly computations repeatedly. Instead of calling the exponential/divide function for each pixel, we perform it only once for each possible pixel value (256 times) and store the result in a table. Thus, we save the CPU time at the cost of a bit of memory. While this may not make a great difference for the standard PC with small image sizes, this makes a huge difference for CPU-limited hardware, such as the Raspberry Pi. In our case, if we want to apply our function for each pixel, we need to make the width by calculating the height; in 100 x 100 pixels, there are 10,000 calculations, but there are only 256 possible values for a pixel. We can then precalculate the pixel values and save them in a LUT vector.

In our sample code, we define the E variable and create a `lut` matrix of 1 row and 256 columns. Then, we do a loop over all possible pixel values by applying our formula and saving them in the `lut` variable:

```
const double exponential_e = std::exp(1.0);
    // Create Lookup table for color curve effect
    Mat lut(1, 256, CV_8UC1);
    Uchar* plut= lut.data;
    for (int i=0; i<256; i++)
    {
        double x= (double)i/256.0;
        plut[i]= cvRound( 256.0 * (1.0/(1.0 + pow(exponential_e, -
        ((x-0.5)/0.1)) )) );
    }
```

As mentioned earlier, in this section we don't apply the function to all channels. We need to split our input image by channels using the `split` function:

```
    // Split the image channels and apply curve transform only to red
channel
    vector<Mat> bgr;
    split(img, bgr);
```

We then apply our `lut` table variable to the red channel. OpenCV give us the LUT function that has the following three parameters:

- An input image
- A matrix of a look up table
- An output image

Then, our call to the LUT function and red channels looks like this:

```
LUT(bgr[2], lut, bgr[2]);
```

Now, we only have to merge our computed channels:

```
// merge result
    merge(bgr, result);
```

The first step is done, and we only have to create the dark halo to finish our effect. Then, we create a gray image with a white circle inside with the same input image size:

```
// Create image for halo dark
    Mat halo( img.rows, img.cols, CV_32FC3, Scalar(0.3,0.3,0.3) );
    // Create circle
    circle(halo, Point(img.cols/2, img.rows/2), img.cols/3,
Scalar(1,1,1), -1);
```

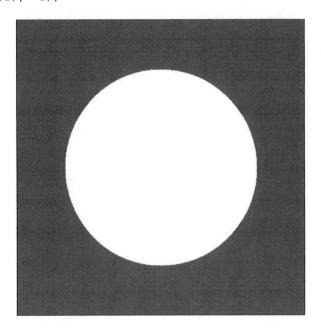

However, if we apply this image to our input image, it will change from dark to white, and we can then apply a big blur using the blur filter function to our circle halo image to get a smooth effect:

```
blur(halo, halo, Size(img.cols/3, img.cols/3));
```

The result after applying the blur filter is shown in the following image:

Now, we need to apply this halo to our image from step 1. An easy way to do this is to multiply both the images. But we need to convert our input image from an 8-bit image to a 32-bit float because we need to multiply our blurred image that has values ranging from 0 to 1 by our input image that has integer values:

```
// Convert the result to float to allow multiply by 1 factor
Mat resultf;
result.convertTo(resultf, CV_32FC3);
```

After we convert our image, we only need to multiply each matrix per element:

```
// Multiply our result with halo
multiply(resultf, halo, resultf);
```

Finally, we convert the float image matrix result to an 8-bit image and show the result:

```
// convert to 8 bits
resultf.convertTo(result, CV_8UC3);

// show result
imshow("Lomograpy", result);
```

The cartoonize effect

In the last section of this chapter, we create another effect called **cartoonize**. The purpose of this effect is to create an image that looks like a cartoon. To do this, we divide the algorithm into two steps: edge detection and color filtering.

The `cartoonCallback` functions define this effect with the following code:

```
void cartoonCallback(int state, void* userData)
{
    /** EDGES **/
    // Apply median filter to remove possible noise
    Mat imgMedian;
    medianBlur(img, imgMedian, 7);

    // Detect edges with canny
    Mat imgCanny;
    Canny(imgMedian, imgCanny, 50, 150);

    // Dilate the edges
    Mat kernel= getStructuringElement(MORPH_RECT, Size(2,2));
    dilate(imgCanny, imgCanny, kernel);
```

```
        // Scale edges values to 1 and invert values
        imgCanny= imgCanny/255;
        imgCanny= 1-imgCanny;

        // Use float values to allow multiply between 0 and 1
        Mat imgCannyf;
        imgCanny.convertTo(imgCannyf, CV_32FC3);

        // Blur the edgest to do smooth effect
        blur(imgCannyf, imgCannyf, Size(5,5));

        /** COLOR **/
        // Apply bilateral filter to homogenizes color
        Mat imgBF;
        bilateralFilter(img, imgBF, 9, 150.0, 150.0);

        // truncate colors
        Mat result= imgBF/25;
        result= result*25;

        /** MERGES COLOR + EDGES **/
        // Create a 3 channles for edges
        Mat imgCanny3c;
        Mat cannyChannels[]={ imgCannyf, imgCannyf, imgCannyf};
        merge(cannyChannels, 3, imgCanny3c);

        // Convert color result to float
        Mat resultf;
        result.convertTo(resultf, CV_32FC3);

        // Multiply color and edges matrices
        multiply(resultf, imgCanny3c, resultf);

        // convert to 8 bits color
        resultf.convertTo(result, CV_8UC3);

        // Show image
        imshow("Result", result);

    }
```

Let's try to understand the code.

The first step is to detect the most important edges of the image. We need to remove noise from the input image before we detect the edges. There are several ways and methods to do this. We will use a median filter to remove any possible small noise, but we can use other methods such as Gaussian blur and so on. The OpenCV function is called `medianBlur` and accepts three parameters: an input image, an output image, and the kernel size (a kernel is a small matrix used to apply some mathematical operation such as convolutional to an image).

```
Mat imgMedian;
medianBlur(img, imgMedian, 7);
```

After removing any possible noise, we detect the strong edges with a `canny` filter:

```
// Detect edges with canny
Mat imgCanny;
Canny(imgMedian, imgCanny, 50, 150);
```

The `canny` filter accepts the following parameters:

- An input image
- An output image
- The first threshold
- The second threshold
- The Sobel size aperture
- The Boolean value to check whether to use a more accurate image gradient magnitude

The smallest value between the first and second threshold is used for edge linking. The largest value is used to find initial segments of strong edges. The `solbel` size aperture is the kernel size of the `sobel` filter that will be used in the algorithm.

After detecting the edges, we will apply a small dilation to join the broken edges:

```
// Dilate the edges
Mat kernel= getStructuringElement(MORPH_RECT, Size(2,2));
dilate(imgCanny, imgCanny, kernel);
```

Similar to what we did in the Lomography effect, we need to multiply our edges' result image by the color image. Then, we require a pixel value between 0 and 1, and so we divide the canny result by 256 and invert the edges to black:

```
// Scale edges values to 1 and invert values
imgCanny= imgCanny/255;
imgCanny= 1-imgCanny;
```

Transform the Canny 8 unsigned bit format to a float matrix:

```
// Use float values to allow multiply between 0 and 1
Mat imgCannyf;
imgCanny.convertTo(imgCannyf, CV_32FC3);
```

To give a cool result, we can blur the edges to give a smooth result line, and then we apply a blur filter:

```
// Blur the edgest to do smooth effect
    blur(imgCannyf, imgCannyf, Size(5,5));
```

The first step of the algorithm is complete, and now we will work with the color.

To get a cartoon look and feel, we will use the bilateral filter:

```
// Apply bilateral filter to homogenizes color
    Mat imgBF;
    bilateralFilter(img, imgBF, 9, 150.0, 150.0);
```

A bilateral filter is a filter used to reduce the noise of an image while keeping edges, but we can get a cartoonish effect with appropriate parameters that we will explore later.

The bilateral filter parameters are as follows:

- An input image
- An output image
- The diameter of a pixel neighborhood; if it's set to negative, it is computed from a sigma space value
- A sigma color value
- A sigma coordinate space

 With a diameter greater than 5, the bilateral filter becomes slow. With sigma values greater than 150, a cartoonish effect appears.

To create a stronger cartoonish effect, we truncate the possible color values to 10 by dividing and multiplying the pixel values. For other values, and to better understand the sigma parameters, read the OpenCV documentation:

```
// truncate colors
    Mat result= imgBF/25;
    result= result*25;
```

Finally, we need to merge the color and edges' results. Then, we need to create a 3-channel image from the first step:

```
// Create a 3 channles for edges
    Mat imgCanny3c;
    Mat cannyChannels[]={ imgCannyf, imgCannyf, imgCannyf};
    merge(cannyChannels, 3, imgCanny3c);
```

Then, we convert our color result image to a 32 float image and then multiply both the images per element:

```
    // Convert color result to float
    Mat resultf;
    result.convertTo(resultf, CV_32FC3);

    // Multiply color and edges matrices
    multiply(resultf, imgCanny3c, resultf);
```

Finally, we only need to convert our image to an 8-bit image and show the resulting image to the user:

```
// convert to 8 bits color
    resultf.convertTo(result, CV_8UC3);

    // Show image
    imshow("Result", result);
```

In the following image, we can see the input image (the left-hand side image) and the result after applying the cartoonize effect (the right-hand side image):

Summary

In this chapter, we learned how to create a complete project that manipulates images after applying different effects. We also split a color image in multiple matrices in order to apply effects to only one channel. We learned how to create look up tables, merge multiple matrices in one, use a canny and bilateral filter, draw circles, and multiply images to perform halo effects.

In the next chapter, we will learn how to do object inspection and how to segment an image in different parts and detect it.

5
Automated Optical Inspection, Object Segmentation, and Detection

In the previous chapter, we learned about histograms and filters that allowed us to understand image manipulation and create a photo application.

In this chapter, we will introduce you to the basic concepts of object segmentation and detection, which means isolation the objects that appear in an image for future processing and analysis.

In this chapter, we will cover the following topics:

- Noise removal
- The basics of light/background removal
- The thresholding operation
- A connected component for object segmentation
- Finding contours for object segmentation

The industry sector uses complex Computer Vision systems and hardware. Computer Vision tries to detect the problems and minimizes errors produced in the production process and increases the quality of final products.

In this sector, the name for Computer Vision tasks is **Automated Optical Inspection** or AOI. This name appears in the inspection of printed circuit board manufacturers, where one or more cameras scan each circuit to detect critical failures and quality defects. This nomenclature was used by other manufacturers to use optical camera systems and Computer Vision algorithms to increase the product quality. Nowadays, the use of optical inspection using different camera types such as infrared, 3D cameras, and so on depends on the problem requirements, such as measure objects, detect surface effects, and so on; and complex algorithms are used in thousands of industries for different purposes, such as defects detection, recognition, classification, and so on.

Isolating objects in a scene

In this section, we will introduce you to the first step of any AOI algorithm, that is, isolating different parts or objects in a scene.

We will take the example of object detection and classification of three object types: a screw, a packing ring, and a nut and develop these in this chapter and *Chapter 6, Learning Object Classification*.

Let's say we are in a company that produces these three objects. All of them are in the same carrier tape, and our objective is to detect each object in the carrier tape and classify each one to allow a robot to put each object on the correct shelf:

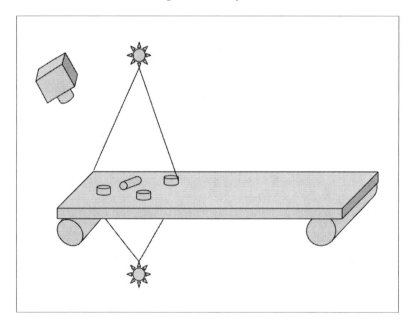

In this chapter, we will isolate each object and detect its position in the image in pixels. In the next chapter, we will classify each isolated object to check whether it is a nut, a screw, or a packing ring.

In the following image, we show our desired result where there are a few objects in the left-hand side image, and in the right-hand side image, we draw each one in different colors. We can show different features such as the area, height, width, countour size, and so on.

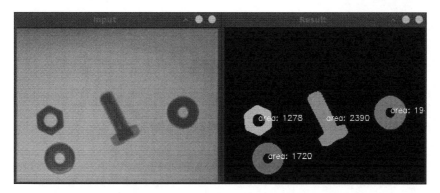

To achieve this result, we will follow different steps that allow us to better understand and organize our algorithm, as shown in the following diagram:

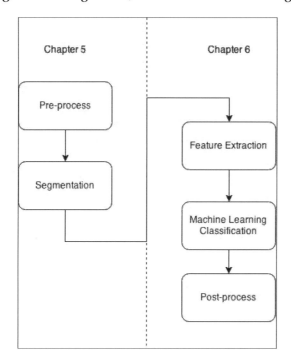

Our application is divided into two chapters. In this chapter, we will develop and understand the preprocessing and segmentation steps. In *Chapter 6, Learning Object Classification,* we will extract the characteristics of each segmented object and train our machine learning system/algorithm to identify each object class to allow you to classify our objects.

Our preprocessing steps are divided into three more substeps, which are as follows:

- Noise removal
- Lighting removal
- Binarization

In the segmentation step, we will use two different algorithms, which are as follows:

- The contour detection algorithm
- The connected component extraction (labeling)

We can see these substeps in the following diagram along with the application flow:

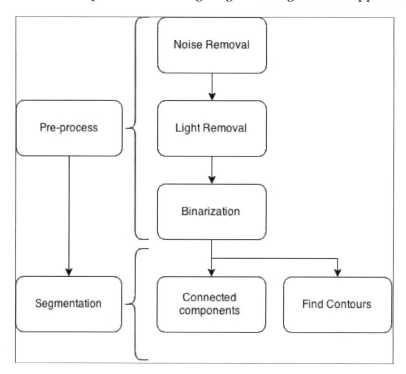

Now, it's time to start the preprocessing step to get the best binarization image by removing the noise and lighting effects in order to minimize the possible detection errors.

Creating an application for AOI

To create our new application, we require a few input parameters when the user executes them; all of them are optional, excluding the input image to be processed:

- An input image to be processed
- The light image pattern
- The light operation, where the user can choose between difference or division operations:
  - If the input value of the user is set to 0, then a difference operation is applied
  - If the input value of the user is set to 1, then a division operation is applied

- Segmentation, where the user can choose between connected components with or without statistics and findContours methods:
  - If the input value of the user is set to 1, then the connected components method for the segment is applied
  - If the input value of the user is set to 2, then the connected components with the statistics area is applied
  - If the input value of the user is set to 3, then the findContours method is applied to the segmentation

To enable this user selection, we will use the command line parser class with these keys:

```
// OpenCV command line parser functions
// Keys accecpted by command line parser
const char* keys =
{
    "{help h usage ? | | print this message}"
    "{@image || Image to process}"
    "{@lightPattern || Image light pattern to apply to image input}"
    "{lightMethod | 1 | Method to remove background light, 0
difference, 1 div }"
    "{segMethod | 1 | Method to segment: 1 connected Components, 2
connected components with stats, 3 find Contours }"
};
```

We use the command line `parser` class that checks the parameters in the `main` function:

```
int main( int argc, const char** argv )
{
  CommandLineParser parser(argc, argv, keys);
  parser.about("Chapter 5. PhotoTool v1.0.0");
  //If requires help show
  if (parser.has("help"))
  {
      parser.printMessage();
      return 0;
  }

  String img_file= parser.get<String>(0);
  String light_pattern_file= parser.get<String>(1);
  int method_light= parser.get<int>("lightMethod");
  int method_seg= parser.get<int>("segMethod");

  // Check if params are correctly parsed in his variables
  if (!parser.check())
  {
      parser.printErrors();
      return 0;
  }
```

After `parser` class our command line user data, we check whether the input image is correctly loaded, and then we load the image and check whether it has data:

```
// Load image to process
  Mat img= imread(img_file, 0);
  if(img.data==NULL){
    cout << "Error loading image "<< img_file << endl;
    return 0;
  }
```

Now, we are ready to create our AOI process of segmentation. We will start with the preprocessing task.

Preprocessing the input image

This section introduces you to some of the most common techniques that can be applied to preprocess images in the context of object segmentation/detection. The preprocess is the first change that we make in a new image before we start with our work and extract the information that we require from it.

Normally, in the preprocessing step, we try to minimize the image noise, light conditions, or image deformations due to the camera lens. These steps minimize the errors when you try to detect objects or segment our image.

Noise removal

If we don't remove the noise, we can detect more objects than we expect because normally noise is represented as a small point in the image and can be segmented as an object. The sensor and scanner circuit normally produce this noise. This variation of brightness or color can be represented in different types, such as Gaussian noise, spike noise, and shot noise. There are different techniques that can be used to remove the noise. We will use a smooth operation, but depending of the type on the noise, we will use some that are better than others. For example, a median filter is normally used to remove the salt-pepper noise:

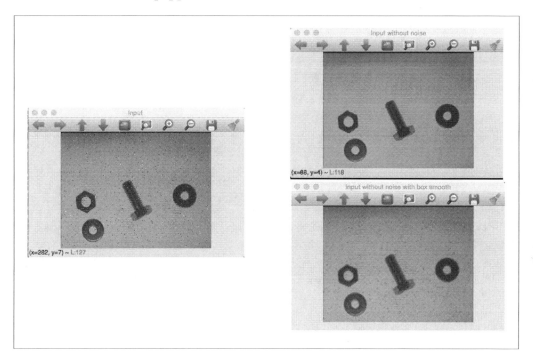

The left-hand side image is the original input with a salt-pepper noise. If we apply a median blur, we get an awesome result where we lose small details. For example, the borders of a screw for which we maintain the perfect edges. Refer to the top-right figure. If we apply a box filter or a Gaussian filter, the noise if not removed. It is just smoothed and the details of objects are loosed and smoothed as well. Refer to the bottom-right figure.

OpenCV provides us with the `medianBlur` function that requires the following three parameters:

- An input image with a 1, 3, or 4 channel image. When the kernel size is greater than 5, the image depth can only be `CV_8U`.

- An output image,which is the resulting image, that has the same type and depth as that of the input.

- The kernel size that has the aperture size greater than 1 and an odd value. For example, 3, 5, 7.

This piece of code used to remove the noise looks like this:

```
Mat img_noise;
medianBlur(img, img_noise, 3);
```

Removing the background using the light pattern for segmentation

In this section, we will develop a basic algorithm that enables us to remove the background using a light pattern. This preprocessing gives us better segmentation. Refer to the following figures. The top-left figure is the input image without noise, and the top-right figure is the result of applying a thresholding operation; we can see the top artifact. The bottom-left figure is the input image after the removal of the background, the bottom-right figure is the thresholding result where there are no artifacts in it and it's better to segment it.

How can we remove the light from our image? It is very simple; we only need a picture of our scenario without any object that is taken from exactly the same position from where the other images have been taken, and to have the same light conditions. This is a very common technique in AOI because the external conditions are supervised and known. The image result of our case is similar to the following figure:

Then, with a simple mathematical operation, we can remove this light pattern. There are two options to remove it, which are as follows:

- Difference
- Division

The difference images are the simplest approach. If we have the light pattern L and the image picture I, the removal R result is the difference between them:

```
R= L-I
```

This division is a bit more complex but simple at the same time. If we have the light pattern matrix L and the image picture matrix I, the removal R result is as follows:

```
R= 255*(1-(I/L))
```

In this case, we divide the image by the light pattern. We make the assumption that if our light pattern is white and the objects are darker than the background carrier tape, then the image pixel values will always remain the same or will be lower than the light pixel values. Then, the result that we obtain from I/L is between 0 and 1. Finally, we invert the result of this division to get the same color direction range and multiply it by 255 to get values between the `0-255` range.

In our code, we will create a new function called `removeLight` with the following parameters:

- An input image to remove the light/background
- Light pattern mat
- Method, `0` is difference, `1` division

The output is a new image matrix without the light/background.

The following code implements the background removal using the light pattern:

```
Mat removeLight(Mat img, Mat pattern, int method)
{
  Mat aux;
  // if method is normalization
  if(method==1)
  {
    // Require change our image to 32 float for division
    Mat img32, pattern32;
    img.convertTo(img32, CV_32F);
    pattern.convertTo(pattern32, CV_32F);
    // Divide the image by the pattern
    aux= 1-(img32/pattern32);
```

```
    // Scale it to convert to 8bit format
    aux=aux*255;
    // Convert 8 bits format
    aux.convertTo(aux, CV_8U);
  }else{
    aux= pattern-img;
  }
  return aux;
}
```

Let's try to understand this. After creating the `aux` variable, in order to save the result, we select the method that is chosen by the user and passed via a parameter to the function. If the method selected is 1, we apply the `division` method.

The `division` method requires a 32-bit float image to allow us to divide the images. The first step is to convert the image and light pattern mat to 32-bit depth:

```
// Require change our image to 32 float for division
Mat img32, pattern32;
img.convertTo(img32, CV_32F);
pattern.convertTo(pattern32, CV_32F);
```

Now we can perform the mathematical operations in our matrix, as described, dividing the image by the pattern and inverting the result:

```
// Divide the image by the pattern
aux= 1-(img32/pattern32);
// Scale it to convert o 8bit format
aux=aux*255;
```

Now, we have the result, but we need to return an 8-bit depth image, and then, use the `convert` function, as we did previously, to convert it to a 32-bit float:

```
// Convert 8 bits format
aux.convertTo(aux, CV_8U);
```

Now we can return the `aux` variable with the result. For the difference method, the development is very easy because we don't have to convert our images, we only need to perform the difference and return. If we don't assume that the pattern is equal to or greater than the image, then we will require a few checks and truncate values that can be less than 0 or greater than 255:

```
aux= pattern-img;
```

The following figure is the result of applying the image light pattern to our input image:

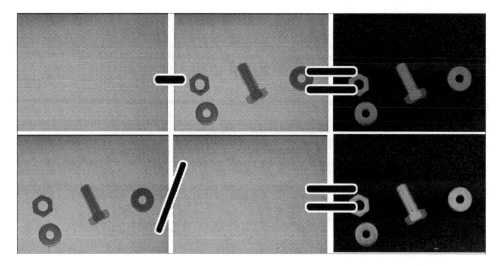

In the results that we obtain, we can check how the light gradient is removed and the possible artifacts are removed as well.

However, what happens when we don't have a light/background pattern? There are a few different techniques to do this, and we are going to present the most basic one. Using a filter, we can create one that can be used, but there are better algorithms from which you can learn the background from a few images, where the pieces appear in different areas. This technique sometimes requires a background estimation image initialization, where our basic approach can play very well. These advanced techniques are explored in the video surveillance chapter.

To estimate the background image, we will use a blur with a large kernel size that is applied to our input image. This is a common technique used in OCR where the letters are thin and small relative to the whole document, and allows us to perform an approximation of the light patterns in the image. We can see the light/background pattern reconstruction on the left-hand side figure and the ground truth on the right-hand side figure:

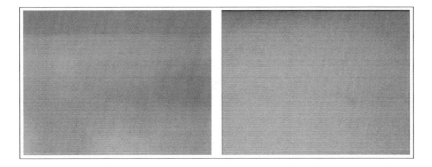

We can see that there are minor differences in the light patterns, but this result is enough to remove the background, and we can see the result in the following figure using difference images.

In the following figure, we can see the result of applying the image difference between the original input image and the estimated background image that are computed with the previous approach:

The `calculateLightPattern` function creates this light pattern or background approximation:

```
Mat calculateLightPattern(Mat img)
{
  Mat pattern;
  // Basic and effective way to calculate the light pattern from one
image
  blur(img, pattern, Size(img.cols/3,img.cols/3));
  return pattern;
}
```

This `basic` function applies a blur to an input image using a big kernel size relative to the image size. From the code, it is one-third of the original width and height.

The thresholding operation

After removing the background, we only have to binarize the image for future segmentation. Now, we will apply the `threshold` function using two different threshold values: a very low value when we remove the light/background because all non-interest regions are black or very low values, and a medium value when we do not use a light removal method because we have a white background and the object images have lower values. This last option allows us to check the results with and without the background removal:

```
// Binarize image for segment
Mat img_thr;
if(method_light!=2){
  threshold(img_no_light, img_thr, 30, 255, THRESH_BINARY);
}else{
  threshold(img_no_light, img_thr, 140, 255, THRESH_BINARY_INV);
}
```

Now, we will continue with the most important part of our application: the segmentation. We will use two different approaches or algorithms: connected components and contours.

Segmenting our input image

Now, we will introduce you to the following two techniques used to segment our thresholded image:

- The connected components
- The `findContours` function

With these two techniques, we will be allowed to extract each region of interest of our image where our target objects appear; in our case, a nut, screw, and ring.

The connected component algorithm

The connected component is a very common algorithm used to segment and identify parts in binary images. A connected component is an iterative algorithm used for the purpose of labeling an image using an 8- or 4-connectivity pixel. Two pixels are connected if they have the same value and are neighbors. In the following figure, each pixel has eight neighbor pixels:

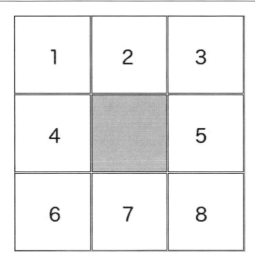

A 4-connectivity means that only the 2, 4, 5, and 7 neighbors can be connected to the center if they have the same value. In the case of 8-connectivity, 1, 2, 3, 4, 5, 6, 7, and 8 can be connected if they have the same value.

In the following example, we can see the difference between an eight and four connectivity algorithm. We will apply each algorithm to the next binarized image. We used a small 9 X 9 image and zoomed it to show how connected components, and the difference between an 4- and 8-connectivity, work:

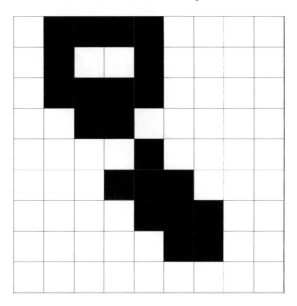

The 4-connectivity algorithm detects two objects, as shown on the left-hand side image. The 8-connectivity algorithm detects only one object (the right-hand side image) because two diagonal pixels are connected, whereas in a 4-connectivity algorithm, only vertical and horizontal pixels are connected. We can see the result in the following figure, where each object has a different gray color value:

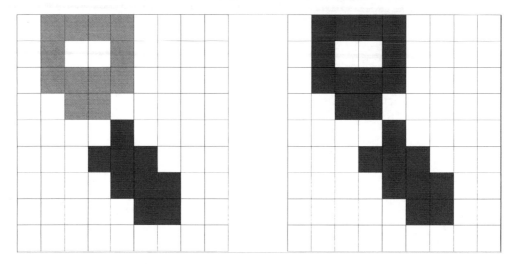

OpenCV 3 introduces you to the connected components algorithm with the following two different functions:

- `connectedComponents(image, labels, connectivity=8, type=CV_32S)`
- `connectedComponentsWithStats(image, labels, stats, centroids, connectivity=8, ltype=CV_32S)`

Both the functions return an integer with the number of detected labels, where the label 0 represents the background.

The difference between these two functions is basically the information that returns each one. Let's check the parameters of each one. The `connectedComponents` function give us the following parameters:

- **Image**: This is the input image to be labeled.
- **Labels**: This is a mat output with the same size of an input image, where each pixel has the value of its label, and all 0's represent the background, the pixels that have 1 as values represent the first connected component object, and so on.
- **Connectivity**: This has two possible values: 8 or 4 that represents the connectivity we want to use.

- **Type**: This is the type of the label image that we would want to use: only two types are allowed, CV32_S or CV16_U. By default, it is CV32_S.

The connectedComponentsWithStats function has two more parameters that are defined: stats and centroids parameters:

- Stats: This is an output parameter for each label, including the background label. The following statistics values can be accessed via stats (label, column), where columns are defined as well, as follows:
    - CC_STAT_LEFT: This is the leftmost x coordinate of a connected component object
    - CC_STAT_TOP: This is the topmost y coordinate of a connected component object
    - CC_STAT_WIDTH: This is the width of a connected component object defined by its bounding box
    - CC_STAT_HEIGHT: This is the height of a connected component object defined by its bounding box
    - CC_STAT_AREA: This is the number of pixels (area) of the connected component object

- Centroids: The centroid points in float type for each label inclusive of the background

In our example application, we will create two functions that are to be applied to these two OpenCV algorithms and show the user the obtained result in a new image with colored objects in the basic algorithm and draw the area of the stats algorithm for each object.

Let's define the basic drawing of the connected component function:

```
void ConnectedComponents(Mat img)
{
  // Use connected components to divide our possibles parts of images
  Mat labels;
  int num_objects= connectedComponents(img, labels);
  // Check the number of objects detected
  if(num_objects < 2 ){
    cout << "No objects detected" << endl;
    return;
  }else{
    cout << "Number of objects detected: " << num_objects - 1 << endl;
  }
```

```
    // Create output image coloring the objects
    Mat output= Mat::zeros(img.rows,img.cols, CV_8UC3);
    RNG rng( 0xFFFFFFFF );
    for(int i=1; i<num_objects; i++){
      Mat mask= labels==i;
      output.setTo(randomColor(rng), mask);
    }
    imshow("Result", output);
  }
```

First of all, we call the OpenCV `connectedComponents` function that returns the number of objects detected. If the number of objects is less than two, this means that only the background object is detected, and then, we don't need to draw anything and finish. If the algorithm detects more than one object, then we show the number of objects detected via the terminal:

```
  Mat labels;
    int num_objects= connectedComponents(img, labels);
    // Check the number of objects detected
    if(num_objects < 2 ){
      cout << "No objects detected" << endl;
      return;
    }else{
      cout << "Number of objects detected: " << num_objects - 1 << endl;
```

Now, we will draw all the detected objects in a new image with different colors, and then we need to create a new black image with the same input size and three channels:

```
  Mat output= Mat::zeros(img.rows,img.cols, CV_8UC3);
```

Then, we need to loop over each label, except the *0* value because it's the background label:

```
  for(int i=1; i<num_objects; i++){
```

To extract each object from the label image, we need to create a mask for each label `i` using a comparison, and save it in a new image:

```
    Mat mask= labels==i;
```

Finally, we set a pseudo-random color to the output image using the mask:

```
    output.setTo(randomColor(rng), mask);
  }
```

After we loop all images, we have all the objects with different colors in our output image, and we only have to show the output image:

```
mshow("Result", output);
```

This is the result where each object is painted with a different color or gray value:

Now, we will explain how to use the connected components with the stats OpenCV algorithm and show some more information in the output result image. The following function implements this functionality:

```
void ConnectedComponentsStats(Mat img)
{
  // Use connected components with stats
  Mat labels, stats, centroids;
  int num_objects= connectedComponentsWithStats(img, labels, stats,
centroids);
  // Check the number of objects detected
  if(num_objects < 2 ){
    cout << "No objects detected" << endl;
    return;
  }else{
    cout << "Number of objects detected: " << num_objects - 1 << endl;
  }
  // Create output image coloring the objects and show area
  Mat output= Mat::zeros(img.rows,img.cols, CV_8UC3);
  RNG rng( 0xFFFFFFFF );
  for(int i=1; i<num_objects; i++){
    cout << "Object "<< i << " with pos: " << centroids.at<Point2d>(i)
<< " with area " << stats.at<int>(i, CC_STAT_AREA) << endl;
    Mat mask= labels==i;
```

```
        output.setTo(randomColor(rng), mask);
        // draw text with area
        stringstream ss;
        ss << "area: " << stats.at<int>(i, CC_STAT_AREA);

        putText(output,
          ss.str(),
          centroids.at<Point2d>(i),
          FONT_HERSHEY_SIMPLEX,
          0.4,
          Scalar(255,255,255));
    }
    imshow("Result", output);
}
```

Let's understand the code, as we did in the non-stats function. We call the connected components algorithm; but, in this case, using the stats function, we check whether we can detect more than one object:

```
Mat labels, stats, centroids;
    int num_objects= connectedComponentsWithStats(img, labels, stats,
centroids);
    // Check the number of objects detected
    if(num_objects < 2 ){
      cout << "No objects detected" << endl;
      return;
    }else{
      cout << "Number of objects detected: " << num_objects - 1 << endl;
    }
```

Now we have two more output results: the stats and centroids variables. Then, for each label that we detect, we will show its centroid and area via the command line:

```
    for(int i=1; i<num_objects; i++){
        cout << "Object "<< i << " with pos: " << centroids.at<Point2d>(i)
<< " with area " << stats.at<int>(i, CC_STAT_AREA) << endl;
```

You can check the call to the stats variable in order to extract the area using the stats.at<int>(I, CC_STAT_AREA) column constant.

Now, as mentioned earlier, we paint the output image of the object labeled with the i number:

```
Mat mask= labels==i;
    output.setTo(randomColor(rng), mask);
```

Finally, we need to add over the image, in the centroid of the object segmented, some info like the area. To do this, we use the `stats` and `centroid` variables using the `putText` function. First, we need to create a stringstream to add the stats area information:

```
// draw text with area
    stringstream ss;
    ss << "area: " << stats.at<int>(i, CC_STAT_AREA);
```

Then, use the `putText` using the centroid as the text position:

```
putText(output,
    ss.str(),
    centroids.at<Point2d>(i),
    FONT_HERSHEY_SIMPLEX,
    0.4,
    Scalar(255,255,255));
```

The result of this function looks like this:

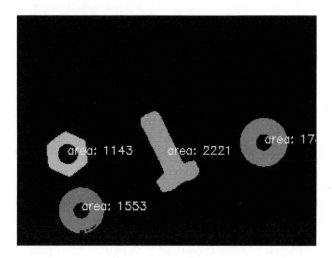

The findContours algorithm

The `findContours` algorithm is one of the most frequently used OpenCV algorithms to segment objects. This algorithm has been included in OpenCV since its first version and provides more information and descriptors, such as shapes, topological organizations, and so on, to the developers:

```
void findContours(InputOutputArray image, OutputArrayOfArrays
contours, OutputArray hierarchy, int mode, int method, Point
offset=Point())
```

Let's explain each parameter, as follows:

- **Image**: This is the input binary image.

- **Contours**: This is the contours output where each detected contour is a vector of points.

- **Hierarchy**: This is the optional output vector where we store the hierarchy of contours. This is the topology of the image where we can get the relations between each contour.

- **Mode**: This is the method used to retrieve the contours:

  ○ `RETR_EXTERNAL`: This retrieves only the external contours.

  ○ `RETR_LIST`: This retrieves all the contours without establishing the hierarchy.

  ○ `RETR_CCOMP`: This retrieves all the contours with two levels of hierarchy: external and holes. If another object is inside one hole, then this is put on the top of the hierarchy.

  ○ `RETR_TREE`: This retrieves all the contours that create a full hierarchy between contours.

- **Method**: This allows you to perform the approximation method to retrieve the contours' shapes:

  ○ `CV_CHAIN_APPROX_NONE`: This does not apply any approximation to the contours and stores all the contours points.

  ○ `CV_CHAIN_APPROX_SIMPLE`: This compresses all the horizontal, vertical, and diagonal segments that store only the start and end points.

  ○ `CV_CHAIN_APPROX_TC89_L1`, `CV_CHAIN_APPROX_TC89_KCOS` This applies the Teh-Chin chain approximation algorithm.

- **Offset**: This is the optional point value used to shift all the contours. This is very useful when we work in a ROI and is required to retrieve the global positions.

Note

The input image is modified by the `findContours` function. Create a copy of your image before it is sent to this function if you need it.

Now that we know the parameters of the findContours function, let's apply them to our example:

```
void FindContoursBasic(Mat img)
{
  vector<vector<Point> > contours;
  findContours(img, contours, RETR_EXTERNAL, CHAIN_APPROX_SIMPLE);
  Mat output= Mat::zeros(img.rows,img.cols, CV_8UC3);
  // Check the number of objects detected
  if(contours.size() == 0 ){
    cout << "No objects detected" << endl;
    return;
  }else{
    cout << "Number of objects detected: " << contours.size() << endl;
  }
  RNG rng( 0xFFFFFFFF );
  for(int i=0; i<contours.size(); i++)
    drawContours(output, contours, i, randomColor(rng));
  imshow("Result", output);
}
```

Let's understand our implementation line by line.

In our case, we don't require any hierarchy, so we will retrieve only the external contours of all possible objects. To do this, we use the RETR_EXTERNAL mode, and we use the basic contour encoding scheme using the CHAIN_APPROX_SIMPLE method:

```
vector<vector<Point> > contours;
vector<Vec4i> hierarchy;
findContours(img, contours, RETR_EXTERNAL, CHAIN_APPROX_SIMPLE);
```

Similar to the connected components examples mentioned earlier, we first check how many contours we have retrieved. If there are none, then we exit from our function:

```
// Check the number of objects detected
  if(contours.size() == 0 ){
    cout << "No objects detected" << endl;
    return;
  }else{
    cout << "Number of objects detected: " << contours.size() << endl;
  }
```

Finally, we draw each detected contour that we detect, and we draw it in our output image with a different color. To do this, OpenCV provides us with a function to draw the result of the find contours image:

```
for(int i=0; i<contours.size(); i++)
    drawContours(output, contours, i, randomColor(rng));
  imshow("Result", output);
}
```

The drawContours function allows the following parameters:

- **Image**: This is the output image used to draw the contours.
- **Contours**: This is the vector of contours.
- **Contour index**: This is a number that indicates the contour to be drawn; if it is negative, all the contours are drawn.
- **Color**: This is the color used to draw the contour.
- **Thickness**: If this is negative, then the contour is filled with the color chosen.
- **Line type**: This is used when we want draw with antialiasing, or other drawing methods.
- **Hierarchy**: This is an optional parameter and is only needed if you want to draw only some of the contours.
- **Max level**: This is an optional parameter and taken into account only when the hierarchy parameter is available. If it is set to 0, only the specified contour is drawn, and if it is set to 1, the function draws the current contour and the nested as well. If it is set to 2, then the algorithm draws all the specified contour hierarchies.
- **Offset**: This is an optional parameter used to shift the contours.

The result of our example can be shown in the following image:

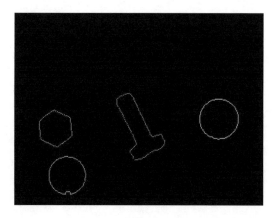

After a binarized image, we can see the three different algorithms that are used to divide and separate each object of an image, allowing us to isolate each object in order to manipulate or extract features.

We can see the entire process in the following image:

Summary

In this chapter, we explored the basics of object segmentation in a controlled situation, where a camera take pictures of different objects.

We learned how to remove the background and light in order to allow us to binarize our image by minimizing the noise and also three different algorithms used to divide and separate each object of an image, allowing us to isolate each object in order to manipulate or extract features. Finally, we extracted all the objects on an image, where we are going to extract characteristics of each of these objects to train a machine learning system.

In the next chapter, we are going to predict the class of any of objects in an image, and then call to a robot or any other system to pick any of them, or detect an object that is not in the correct carrier tape, and then notify to a person to pick it up.

Learning Object Classification

6

In the previous chapter, we introduced you to the basic concepts of object segmentation and detection. This means isolating the objects that appear in an image for future processing and analysis.

This chapter covers how to classify each of these isolated objects. In order to allow us to classify each object, we need to train our system to be capable of learning the required parameters to decide which specific label should be assigned to the detected object (depending on the different categories taken into account during the training phase).

This chapter is going to introduce you to the basic concepts of machine learning to classify images with different labels.

We will create a basic application based on the segmentation algorithm, as discussed in *Chapter 5, Automated Optical Inspection, Object Segmentation, and Detection*. This segmentation algorithm extracts parts of an image, which contains objects. For each object, we will extract the different features and analyze them using a machine learning algorithm. Using a machine learning algorithm, we are able to show, using our user interface, the labels of each object detected in the input image to the end user.

In this chapter, we will cover the different topics and algorithms, which are as follows:

- An introduction to machine learning concepts
- Common machine learning algorithms and processes
- Feature extraction
- Support vector machines
- Training and prediction

Introducing machine learning concepts

Machine learning is an old concept that was defined in 1959 by Arthur Samuel as a *field of study that gives computers the ability to learn without being explicitly programmed.* Tom. M. Mitchel provided a more formal definition. In this definition, Tom links the concept of samples or experiences, labels, and performance measurements.

> The machine learning definition by Arthur Samuel is referenced from *Some Studies in Machine Learning Using the Game of Checkers* in the *IBM Journal of Research and Development* (Volume: 3, Issue: 3), p. 210 and a phrase in *The New Yorker* and *Office Management* the same year.
>
> The more formal definition by Tom. M. Mitchel is referenced from *Machine Learning Book*, McGray Hill 1997 (http://www.cs.cmu.edu/afs/cs.cmu.edu/user/mitchell/ftp/mlbook.html).

Machine learning involves pattern recognition and the learning theory in artificial intelligence and is related to computational statistics.

Machine learning is used in hundreds of applications such as **OCR (Optical Character Recognition)**, spam filtering, search engines, and thousands of Computer Vision applications that we will develop in the current chapter, where a machine learning algorithm tries to classify the objects that appear in the input image.

Depending on how machine ML algorithms learn from the data or samples, we can divide them into three categories, which are as follows:

- **Supervised learning**: The computer learns from a set of labeled data. The goal is to learn the parameters of the model and rules that allow computers to map the relation between data and output label results.

- **Unsupervised learning**: No labels are given, and the computer tries to discover the input structure of the input data.

- **Reinforcement learning**: The computer interacts with a dynamic environment that performs its goal and learns from its mistakes.

Depending on the desired results that we obtain from our machine learning algorithm, we can categorize them into the following:

- **Classification**: In classification, the space of the inputs can be divided into N classes, and the prediction results of a given sample are one of these training classes. This is one of the most used categories. A typical example is an e-mail spam filtering where there are only two classes: spam and non spam or OCR, where only N characters are available, and each character is one class.

- **Regression**: The output is a continuous value instead of a discrete value such as a classification result. One example of regression can be the prediction of the house price by providing the house size, number of years, and location.

- **Clustering**: The inputs are divided into N groups using unsupervised training.

- **Density estimation**: This finds the (probability) distribution of inputs.

In our example, we will use a supervised learning classification algorithm, where a training dataset (with labels) is used to train the model, and the result of our model is a prediction of one label.

Machine learning is a modern approach to artificial intelligence and statistics and involves both the techniques.

In machine learning, there are several approaches and methods, and some of them used are **SVM (support vector machines)**, **ANNs (artificial neural networks)**, clustering such as **K-Nearest Neighbors**, **decision trees,** or deep learning, which is a big **neural network** approach used in some cases that are convolutional, and so on.

All these methods and approaches are supported, implemented, and well-documented in OpenCV. We are going to explain one of them, SVM, in the next section.

OpenCV implements eight of these machine learning algorithms. They all inherit from the `StatModel` class:

- Artificial neural networks
- Boost
- Random trees
- Expectation maximization
- K-Nearest Neighbours
- Logistic regression
- The Normal Bayes Classifier
- Support vector machines

To get more details of each algorithm, read the OpenCV document page of machine learning at http://docs.opencv.org/trunk/dc/dd6/ ml_intro.html.

In the following image, you can see the machine learning class hierarchy:

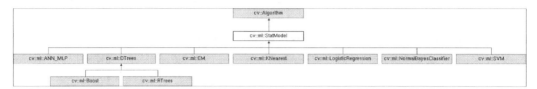

The StatModel class provides all the read and write functions that are very important to save our machine learning parameters and training data.

In machine learning, the most time-consuming part is the training method. Training can take from seconds to weeks or months for large datasets and complex machine learning structures; for example, in deep learning and a big neural network structure with more than 100,000 images. In deep learning algorithms, it is common to use parallel hardware processing; for example, GPUs or graphic cards with the CUDA technology used to decrease the computing time during training.

This means that we cannot train our algorithm each time we run our application, and it's recommended that we save our model after it is trained because all training/ prediction parameters of machine learning are saved. Next, when we want to run it in the future, we only need to load/read from our saved model without training anymore if we need to update our model with more data.

The StatModel is an interface that is implemented by each of its implementations. The two key functions are train and predict.

The train method is responsible for learning the parameters of the model from a training dataset. The train function has the following four calls that can be called in four different ways:

```
bool train(const Ptr<TrainData>& trainData, int flags=0 );
bool train(InputArray samples, int layout, InputArray responses);
Ptr<_Tp> train(const Ptr<TrainData>& data, const _Tp::Params& p, int
flags=0 );
Ptr<_Tp> train(InputArray samples, int layout, InputArray responses,
const _Tp::Params& p, int flags=0 );
```

It has the following parameters:

- `trainData`: This is the training data that can be loaded or created from the `TrainData` class. This class is new in OpenCV 3 and helps developers to create training data because different algorithms require different types of structure of arrays for training and prediction, such as the ANN algorithm.
- `samples`: This is the array of training array samples such as training data in the format required by the machine learning algorithm.
- `layout`: There are two types of layouts: `ROW_SAMPLE` (training samples are the matrix rows) and `COL_SAMPLE` (training samples are the matrix columns).
- `responses`: This is the vector of responses that is associated with the sample data.
- `p`: This is the `StatModel` parameter.
- `flags`: These are optional flags defined by each method.

The `predict` method is simpler and has only one call:

```
float StatModel::predict(InputArray samples, OutputArray
results=noArray(), int flags=0 )
```

It has the following parameters:

- `samples`: These are the input samples to be predicted. There can be only one or multiple data to be predicted.
- `results`: This is the result of each input row samples (computed by the algorithm from the previously trained model).
- `flags`: These are optional flags that are model-dependent. Some models, such as Boost and SVM recognize the `StatModel::RAW_OUTPUT` flag, which makes the method return the raw results (the sum) and not the class label.

The `StatModel` class provides other very useful methods, which are as follows:

- `isTrained()`: This returns `true` if the model is trained
- `isClassifier()`: This returns `true` if the model is a classifier or `false` in the case of regression
- `getVarCount()`: This returns the number of variables in training samples
- `save(const string& filename)`: This saves the model in the filename
- `Ptr<_Tp> load(const string& filename)`: This loads the model from the filename, for example: `Ptr<SVM> svm = StatModel::load<SVM>("my_svm_model.xml");`

- `calcError(const Ptr<TrainData>& data, bool test, OutputArray resp)`: This calculates the error from a test data, where the data is the training data. If the test is `true`, the method calculates the error from the test subset of all the training data, otherwise it's computed over the training subset of the data. Finally `resp` is the optional output results.

Now, we will learn how to construct a basic application that uses machine learning in Computer Vision apps.

Computer Vision and the machine learning workflow

The Computer Vision applications with machine learning have a common basic structure. This structure is divided into different steps that are repeated in almost all Computer Vision applications, and some others are omitted. In the following diagram, we show you the different steps involved:

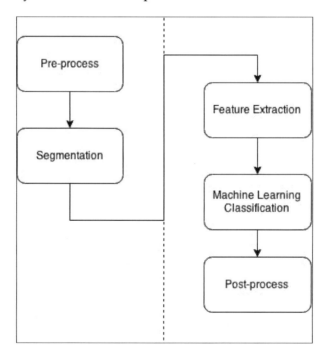

Almost any Computer Vision application starts with a preprocessing stage that is applied to the input image. Preprocessing involves light removal conditions and noise, thresholding, blur, and so on.

After we apply all the preprocessing steps required to the input image, the second step is segmentation. In the segmentation step, we need to extract the regions of interest of an image and isolate each one as a unique object of interest. For example, in a face detection system, we need to separate the faces from the rest of the parts in the scene.

After getting the objects inside the image, we continue with the next step. We need to extract all the features of each one detected object; a feature is a vector of characteristics of objects. A characteristic describes our objects and can be the area of the object, contour, texture pattern, and so on.

Now, we have the descriptor of our object; a descriptor is a feature that describes an object, and we use these descriptors to train our model or predict one of them. To do this, we need to create a big dataset of features, where hundreds, thousands, and millions of images are preprocessed, and extracted features use all these features in a train model function that we choose:

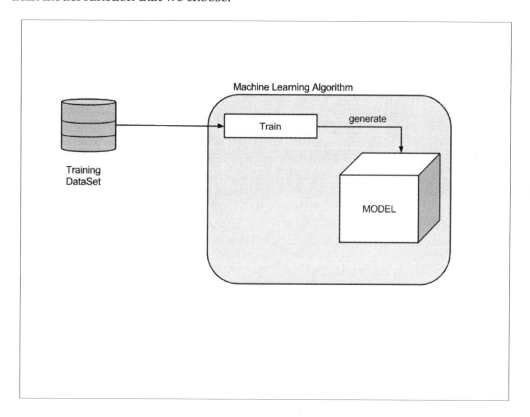

When we train a dataset, the model learns all the parameters required to predict when a new vector of features with an unknown label is given:

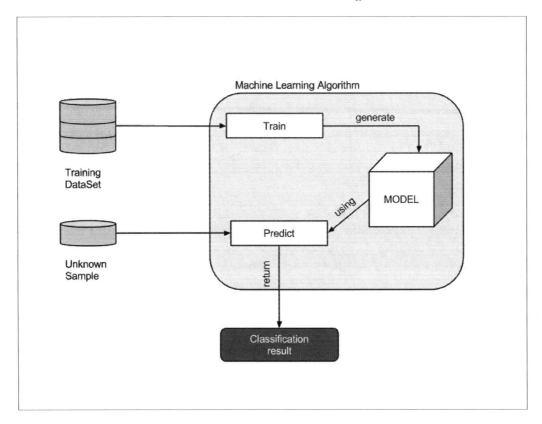

After we get the prediction, sometimes, a post-processing of output data is required; for example, merging multiple classifications to decrease the prediction error or merging multiple labels. A sample case is **OCR (Optical Character Recognition)**, where the classification result is per character, and by combining the results of character recognitions, we construct a word. This means that we can create a post-processing method to correct errors in detected words.

With this small introduction to machine learning for Computer Vision, we will learn how to implement our own application that uses machine learning to classify objects in a slide tape. We will use support vector machines as our classification methods, and see how to use them. The other machine learning algorithms have very similar uses. The OpenCV documentation has a detailed information about all machine learning algorithms.

Automatic object inspection classification example

Continuing with the example of the previous chapter, the automatic object inspection segmentation, where a carrier tape contains three different types of objects (nuts, screws, and rings), and with Computer Vision, we will be able to recognize each one of them to send notifications to a robot or similar to put each one in different boxes.

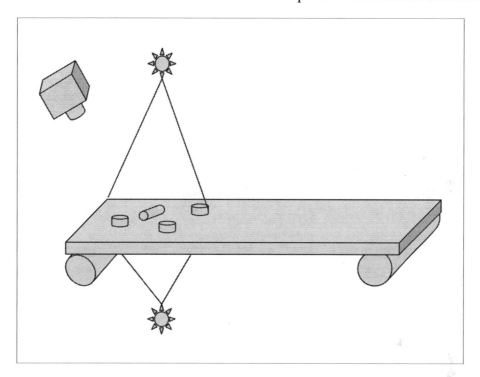

In *Chapter 5, Automated Optical Inspection, Object Segmentation, and Detection,* we preprocessed the input images and extracted the regions of interest of images and isolated each object using different techniques. Now, we will apply all these concepts, as explained in previous sections, in this example to extract features and classify each object and allow to possible robot to put each one in different boxes. In our application, we are only going to show the labels of each image in an image, but we can send the positions in the image and the labels to other devices as a robot.

Then, our goal is from an input image with few objects to show the objects' names over each one, as per the following image. However, to learn all the steps of the complete process, we will train our system to show each image that is trained, create a plot to show each object the features that we are going to use with different colors, the preprocessed input image, and finally, the output classification result with the following result:

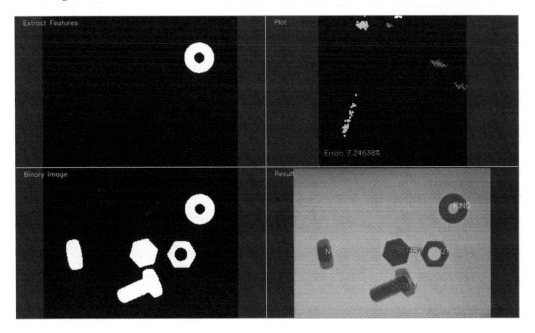

We will perform the following steps for our example application:

1. For training each image:
    ◦   Preprocess an image
    ◦   Segment an image

2. For each object in an image:
    ◦   Extract the features
    ◦   Add the object to the training feature vector with its label

3. Create an SVM model.

4. Train our SVM model with the training feature vector.

5. Preprocess an input image to be classified.

6. Segment an input image.

7. For each object detected:

    ○ Extract the features

    ○ Predict with an SVM model

    ○ Paint the result in an output image

For the preprocessing and segmentation stage, we will use the code discussed in *Chapter 5, Automated Optical Inspection, Object Segmentation, and Detection*, and we will explain how to extract the features and create the vectors required to train and predict our model.

Feature extraction

Now, let's extract the features of each object. To understand the feature concept of a feature vector, we will extract very simple features, but it is enough to get good results. In other solutions, we can get more complex features, such as texture descriptors, contour descriptors, and so on.

In our example, we only have these three types of objects, *nuts*, *rings*, and *screws*, in different possible positions. All these possible objects and positions are shown in the following figure:

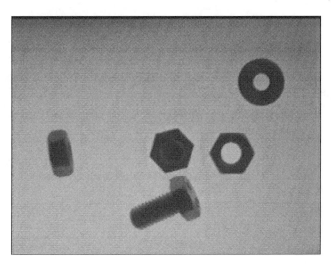

We will explore the good characteristics that will help the computer to identify each object. The characteristics are as follows:

- The area of an object
- The aspect ratio, which is the width divided by the height of the bounding rectangle
- The number of holes
- The number of contour sides

These characteristics can describe our objects very well, and if we use all of them, the classification error can be very small. However, in our implemented example, we will use only the first two characteristics, the area and aspect ratio, for learning purposes because we can plot these characteristics in 2D graphics, and we can show that these values describe our objects correctly. We can differentiate one kind of object from the others visually in the graphic plot.

To extract these features, we will use the black/white input ROI image as the input, where only one object appears in a white color with a black background. This input is the result of segmentation, as discussed in *Chapter 5, Automated Optical Inspection, Object Segmentation, and Detection*. We will use the findCountours algorithm for segmentation objects and create the ExtractFeatures function for this purpose:

```
vector< vector<float> > ExtractFeatures(Mat img, vector<int>*
left=NULL, vector<int>* top=NULL)
{
  vector< vector<float> > output;
  vector<vector<Point> > contours;
  Mat input= img.clone();

  vector<Vec4i> hierarchy;
  findContours(input, contours, hierarchy, RETR_CCOMP, CHAIN_APPROX_
SIMPLE);
  // Check the number of objects detected
  if(contours.size() == 0 ){
    return output;
  }
  RNG rng( 0xFFFFFFFF );
  for(int i=0; i<contours.size(); i++){

    Mat mask= Mat::zeros(img.rows, img.cols, CV_8UC1);
    drawContours(mask, contours, i, Scalar(1), FILLED, LINE_8,
      hierarchy, 1);
```

```
        Scalar area_s= sum(mask);
        float area= area_s[0];

        if(area>500){ //if the area is greather than min.

            RotatedRect r= minAreaRect(contours[i]);
            float width= r.size.width;
            float height= r.size.height;
            float ar=(width<height)?height/width:width/height;

            vector<float> row;
            row.push_back(area);
            row.push_back(ar);
            output.push_back(row);
            if(left!=NULL){
                left->push_back((int)r.center.x);
            }
            if(top!=NULL){
                top->push_back((int)r.center.y);
            }

            miw->addImage("Extract Features", mask*255);
            miw->render();
            waitKey(10);
        }
    }
    return output;
}
```

Let's understand the code in detail.

We will create a function that has one image as the input and returns two vectors of left and top position for each object detected in the image as parameters; this will be used to draw its label over each object. The output of the function is a vector of vectors of floats; in other words, a matrix where each row contains the features of each object that is detected.

Let's create a function that draws a label over each other:

1. Firstly, we need to create the output vector variable and contours variable that are to be used in our `FindContours` algorithm segmentation, and we need to create a copy of our input image because the `findContours` OpenCV functions modify the input image:

```
vector< vector<float> > output;
vector<vector<Point> > contours;
Mat input= img.clone();
vector<Vec4i> hierarchy;
findContours(input, contours, hierarchy, RETR_CCOMP,
    CHAIN_APPROX_SIMPLE);
```

2. Now, we can use the `findContours` function to retrieve each object in an image. If we don't detect any contour, we return an empty output matrix:

```
if(contours.size() == 0 ){
    return output;
}
```

3. For each object `contour` we are going to draw in a black image each object using 1 as the color value. This is our mask image to compute all features:

```
for(int i=0; i<contours.size(); i++){
Mat mask= Mat::zeros(img.rows, img.cols, CV_8UC1);
    drawContours(mask, contours, i, Scalar(1), FILLED, LINE_8,
hierarchy, 1);
```

4. It's important to use the value 1 to draw inside the shape because we can calculate the area by summing all values inside the contour:

```
    Scalar area_s= sum(mask);
    float area= area_s[0];
```

5. This area is our first feature. Now, we will use this area value as a filter to remove the small objects that we need to avoid. All objects with an area less than a minimum area are discarded. After we pass the filter, we create the second feature, that is, the aspect ratio of an object. This means that the maximum width or height is divided by the minimum width or height. This feature can differentiate the screw from other objects easily:

```
if(area>MIN_AREA){ //if the area is greather than min.
    RotatedRect r= minAreaRect(contours[i]);
    float width= r.size.width;
    float height= r.size.height;
    float ar=(width<height)?height/width:width/height;
```

6. Now, we have the features, and we only need to add these features to the output vector. To do this, we create a row vector of floats and add these values, and later on, add this row to the output vector:

```
vector<float> row;
        row.push_back(area);
        row.push_back(ar);
        output.push_back(row);
```

7. If the left and top `params` are passed, then add the top-left values to the `params` output:

```
    if(left!=NULL){
            left->push_back((int)r.center.x);
    }
    if(top!=NULL){
            top->push_back((int)r.center.y);
    }
```

8. Finally, we will show the detected objects in a window for the user feedback, and when we finish processing all the objects in the image, we will return the output feature vector:

```
        miw->addImage("Extract Features", mask*255);
        miw->render();
        waitKey(10);
    }
}
    return output;
```

Now, we can extract the features of each input image, and we need to continue with the next step, which is to train our model.

Training an SVM model

We will use a supervised learning model, and then, we will require images of each object and their corresponding labels. There are no minimum number of images in the dataset. If we provide more images for the training process, we will get a better classification model (in most of the cases), but simple classifiers can be enough to train simple models. To do this, we create three folders (`screw`, `nut`, and `ring`), where all the images of each type are placed together.

For each image in the folder, we need to extract the features and add them to the train feature matrix, and at same time, we need to create a new vector with the labels for each row, corresponding to each training matrix.

To evaluate our system, we split each folder into a number of images for testing and training purposes. We leave around 20 images for testing and the others for training. Then, we need to create two vectors of labels and two matrices for train and test.

Then, let's understand the code. First, we need to create our model. We need to declare the model in order to be able access it as a global variable. OpenCV uses the Ptr template class for pointers:

```
Ptr<SVM> svm;
```

After we declare the pointer to the new SVM model, we need to create it and train it. We create the trainAndTest function for this purpose:

```
void trainAndTest()
{
  vector< float > trainingData;
  vector< int > responsesData;
  vector< float > testData;
  vector< float > testResponsesData;

  int num_for_test= 20;

  // Get the nut images
  readFolderAndExtractFeatures("../data/nut/tuerca_%04d.pgm", 0,
    num_for_test, trainingData, responsesData, testData,
      testResponsesData);
  // Get and process the ring images
  readFolderAndExtractFeatures("../data/ring/arandela_%04d.pgm",
    1, num_for_test, trainingData, responsesData, testData,
      testResponsesData);
  // get and process the screw images
  readFolderAndExtractFeatures("../data/screw/tornillo_%04d.pgm",
    2, num_for_test, trainingData, responsesData, testData,
      testResponsesData);

  cout << "Num of train samples: " << responsesData.size() <<
    endl;

  cout << "Num of test samples: " << testResponsesData.size() <<
    endl;

  // Merge all data
  Mat trainingDataMat(trainingData.size()/2, 2, CV_32FC1,
    &trainingData[0]);
```

```
Mat responses(responsesData.size(), 1, CV_32SC1,
  &responsesData[0]);

Mat testDataMat(testData.size()/2, 2, CV_32FC1, &testData[0]);
Mat testResponses(testResponsesData.size(), 1, CV_32FC1,
  &testResponsesData[0]);

svm = SVM::create();
    svm->setType(SVM::C_SVC);
    svm->setKernel(SVM::CHI2);
    svm->setTermCriteria(TermCriteria(TermCriteria::MAX_ITER,
        100, 1e-6));

svm->train(trainingDataMat, ROW_SAMPLE, responses);

if(testResponsesData.size()>0){
  cout << "Evaluation" << endl;
  cout << "==========" << endl;
  // Test the ML Model
  Mat testPredict;
  svm->predict(testDataMat, testPredict);
  cout << "Prediction Done" << endl;
  // Error calculation
  Mat errorMat= testPredict!=testResponses;
  float error= 100.0f * countNonZero(errorMat) /
    testResponsesData.size();
  cout << "Error: " << error << "\%" << endl;
  // Plot training data with error label
  plotTrainData(trainingDataMat, responses, &error);

}else{
  plotTrainData(trainingDataMat, responses);
}
}
```

Let's understand the code in detail.

First, we need to create the required variables to store the training and test data:

```
vector< float > trainingData;
vector< int > responsesData;
vector< float > testData;
vector< float > testResponsesData;
```

As mentioned earlier, we need to read all the images from each folder, extract the features, and save them in our training and test data. To do this, we will use the `readFolderAndExtractFeatures` function:

```
int num_for_test= 20;
// Get the nut images
readFolderAndExtractFeatures("../data/nut/tuerca_%04d.pgm", 0,
    num_for_test, trainingData, responsesData, testData,
      testResponsesData);
// Get and process the ring images
readFolderAndExtractFeatures("../data/ring/arandela_%04d.pgm",
    1, num_for_test, trainingData, responsesData, testData,
      testResponsesData);
// get and process the screw images
readFolderAndExtractFeatures("../data/screw/tornillo_%04d.pgm",
    2, num_for_test, trainingData, responsesData, testData,
      testResponsesData);
```

The `readFolderAndExtractFeatures` function uses the `VideoCapture` OpenCV function to read all the images of a folder like a video or camera. For each image read, we extract the features and then add them to the corresponding output vector:

```
bool readFolderAndExtractFeatures(string folder, int label, int num_
for_test,
  vector<float> &trainingData, vector<int> &responsesData,
  vector<float> &testData, vector<float> &testResponsesData)
{
  VideoCapture images;
  if(images.open(folder)==false){
    cout << "Can not open the folder images" << endl;
    return false;
  }
  Mat frame;
  int img_index=0;
  while( images.read(frame) ){
    //// Preprocess image
    Mat pre= preprocessImage(frame);
    // Extract features
    vector< vector<float> > features= ExtractFeatures(pre);
    for(int i=0; i< features.size(); i++){
      if(img_index >= num_for_test){
        trainingData.push_back(features[i][0]);
        trainingData.push_back(features[i][1]);
        responsesData.push_back(label);
```

```
    }else{
      testData.push_back(features[i][0]);
      testData.push_back(features[i][1]);
      testResponsesData.push_back((float)label);
    }
  }
  img_index++;
}
return true;
}
```

After filling all the vectors with features and labels, we need to convert them to the OpenCV `mat` format in order to send them to the `training` function:

```
// Merge all data
Mat trainingDataMat(trainingData.size()/2, 2, CV_32FC1,
  &trainingData[0]);
Mat responses(responsesData.size(), 1, CV_32SC1,
  &responsesData[0]);
Mat testDataMat(testData.size()/2, 2, CV_32FC1, &testData[0]);
Mat testResponses(testResponsesData.size(), 1, CV_32FC1,
  &testResponsesData[0]);
```

We are now ready to create and train our machine learning model, as mentioned earlier, and we are going to use a support vector machine. First, we need to set up the basic model parameters:

```
// Set up SVM's parameters
  svm = SVM::create();
svm->setType(SVM::C_SVC);
svm->setKernel(SVM::CHI2);
svm->setTermCriteria(TermCriteria(TermCriteria::MAX_ITER, 100, 1e-6));
```

We need to define the SVM type and kernel to be used and the criteria to stop the learning process; in our case, we will use a maximum number of iterations, stopping at 100 iterations. For more information on each parameter and what it does, check out the OpenCV documentation. After we create the parameters of the setup, we need to create the model by calling the `train` method and using the `trainingDataMat` and response matrices:

```
// Train the SVM
svm->train(trainingDataMat, ROW_SAMPLE, responses);
```

We use the test vector (by setting the `num_for_test` variable greater than 0) to obtain an approximation error of our model. To get the error estimation, we need to predict all the test vector features to obtain the SVM prediction results and then compare these results to the original labels:

```
if (testResponsesData.size()>0){
    cout << "Evaluation" << endl;
    cout << "==========" << endl;
    // Test the ML Model
    Mat testPredict;
    svm->predict(testDataMat, testPredict);
    cout << "Prediction Done" << endl;
    // Error calculation
    Mat errorMat= testPredict!=testResponses;
    float error= 100.0f * countNonZero(errorMat) /
      testResponsesData.size();
    cout << "Error: " << error << "\%" << endl;
    // Plot training data with error label
    plotTrainData(trainingDataMat, responses, &error);
}else{
    plotTrainData(trainingDataMat, responses);
}
```

We use the `predict` function using the `testDataMat` features and a new `mat` to predict results. The `predict` function allows you to do multiple predictions at the same time, giving a matrix instead of only one row.

After the prediction is done, we only need to get the difference of `testPredict` using our `testResponses` (the original labels). If there are differences, we only need to count the number of differences and divide them by the total number of tests to get the error.

We can use the new `TrainData` class to generate the feature vectors and samples and split out train data in test and train vectors.

Finally, we need to show the training data in a 2D plot, where the *y* axis is the aspect ratio feature and the *x* axis is the area of objects. Each point has a different color and shape (cross, square, and circle) that shows a different kind of object, and we can clearly see the groups of objects in the following figure:

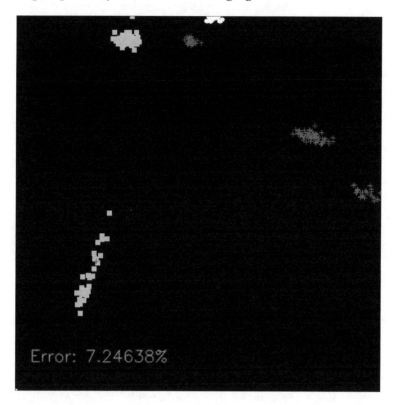

Now, we are very close to finishing our application sample. We have a trained SVM model that we can use as a classification model to detect the type of a new incoming and unknown feature vector. Then, the next step is to predict an input image with unknown objects.

Input image prediction

Now, we are ready to explain the main function, which loads the input image and predicts the objects that appear inside. We are going to use something like this, as shown in the following figure, as the input image where multiple and different objects appear:

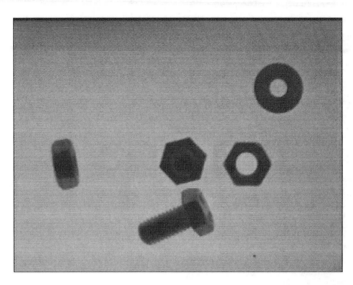

For all training images, we need to load and preprocess the input image:

1. First, we load and convert the images to gray color values.

2. We then apply the preprocessing tasks, as discussed in *Chapter 5,*
   Automated Optical Inspection, Object Segmentation, and Detection, using the
   preprocessImage function:

   ```
   Mat pre= preprocessImage(img);
   ```

3. Now, we extract the features of vectors of all the objects that appear in the
   image and the top-left positions of each one using the ExtractFeatures that
   we mentioned earlier:

   ```
   // Extract features
     vector<int> pos_top, pos_left;
     vector< vector<float> > features= ExtractFeatures(pre, &pos_
   left, &pos_top);
   ```

4. For each object that we detect, we store it as a feature row, and then,
   we convert each row as a Mat of one row and two features:

   ```
   for(int i=0; i< features.size(); i++){
       Mat trainingDataMat(1, 2, CV_32FC1, &features[i][0]);
   ```

5. Then, we predict the single object using the `predict` function of our `StatModel` SVM:

```
float result= svm->predict(trainingDataMat);
```

The float result of the prediction is the label of the object that is detected. Then, to complete the application, we only need to draw the label over each image in an output image.

6. We will use a `stringstream` to store the text and a `Scalar` to store the color of each different label:

```
stringstream ss;
    Scalar color;
    if(result==0){
      color= green; // NUT
      ss << "NUT";
    }
    else if(result==1){
      color= blue; // RING
      ss << "RING" ;
    }
    else if(result==2){
      color= red; // SCREW
      ss << "SCREW";
    }
```

7. Draw the label text over each object using its detected position in the `ExtractFeatures` function:

```
putText(img_output,
        ss.str(),
        Point2d(pos_left[i], pos_top[i]),
        FONT_HERSHEY_SIMPLEX,
        0.4,
        color);
```

8. Finally, we will draw our results in the output window:

```
miw->addImage("Binary image", pre);
miw->addImage("Result", img_output);
miw->render();
waitKey(0);
```

The final result of our application shows a window that is tiled with four screens, where the top-left image is the input training image, the top-right image is the plot training image, the bottom-left image is the input image to analyze preprocessed, and the bottom-right image is the final result of the prediction:

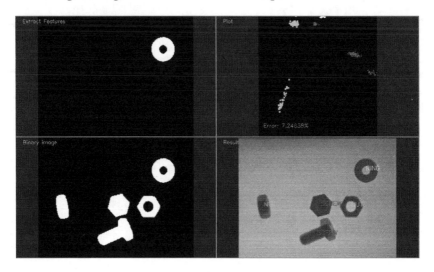

Summary

In this chapter, we learned the basics of the machine learning model and how to apply a small sample application to understand all the basic tips required to create our own ML application.

Machine learning is complex and involves different techniques for each use case (supervised learning, unsupervised, clustering, and so on), and we learned how to create the most typical ML application and the supervised learning with an SVM.

The most important concepts in supervised machine learning are: first, we need to have an appropriate number of samples or datasets; and second, we need to correctly choose the features that describe our objects correctly. For more information on image features, refer to *Chapter 8*, *Video Surveillance, Background Modeling, and Morphological Operations*. Third, choose the best model that gives us the best predictions.

If we don't reach the correct predictions we have to check each one of these concepts to look for where the issue is.

In the next chapter, we will introduce background subtraction methods, which are very useful for video surveillance applications where the backgrounds don't give us any interesting information and must be discarded to allow the segmentation of the interested objects in which to analyze.

7
Detecting Face Parts and Overlaying Masks

In the previous chapter, we learned about object classification and how machine learning can be used to achieve it. In this chapter, we will learn how to detect and track different face parts. We will start the discussion by understanding the face detection pipeline and how it's built from the ground up. We will then use this framework to detect face parts, such as eyes, ears, mouth, and nose. We will then learn how to overlay funny masks on these face parts in a live video.

In this chapter, we will cover the following topics:

- Working with Haar cascades
- Integral images and why we need them
- Building a generic face detection pipeline
- Detecting and tracking face parts, such as eyes, ears, nose, and mouth in a live video stream from the webcam
- Automatically overlaying facemasks, sunglasses, and a funny nose on a person's face in a video

Understanding Haar cascades

Haar cascades are cascade classifiers that are based on Haar features. What is a cascade classifier? It is simply a concatenation of a set of weak classifiers that can be used to create a strong classifier. Now, what do we mean by *weak* and *strong* classifiers? Weak classifiers are classifiers whose performances are limited. They don't have the ability to classify everything correctly. If you keep the problem really simple, they might perform at an acceptable level. Strong classifiers, on the other hand, are really good at classifying our data correctly. We will see how it all comes together in the next couple of paragraphs. Another important part of Haar cascades is *Haar features*. These features are simple summations of rectangles and differences of those areas across the image. Let's consider the following figure:

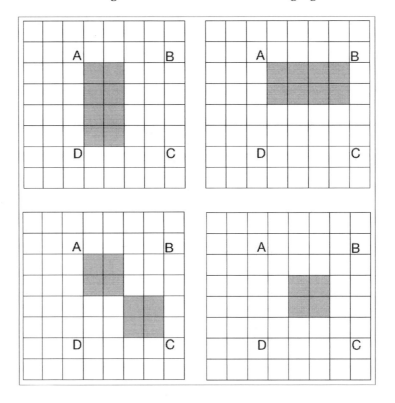

If we want to compute the Haar features of the region ABCD, we just need to compute the difference between the white pixels and the colored pixels in that region. As shown in in the preceding four figures, we use different patterns to build Haar features. There are a lot of other patterns that are used as well. We do this at multiple scales to make the system scale invariant. When we say *multiple scales*, we just scale the image down to compute the same features again. This way, we can make it robust against size variations of a given object.

As it turns out, this concatenation system is a very good method to detect objects in an image. In 2001, *Paul Viola* and *Michael Jones* published a seminal paper where they described a fast and effective method for object detection. If you are curious to learn more about it, you can check out their paper at `http://www.cs.ubc.ca/~lowe/425/slides/13-ViolaJones.pdf`.

Let's dive deeper into it to understand what they actually did. They basically described an algorithm that uses a boosted cascade of simple classifiers. This system is used to build a strong classifier that can perform really well. Why did they use these simple classifiers instead of complex classifiers that can be more accurate? Well, using this technique, they were able to avoid the problem of having to build a single classifier that can perform with high precision. These single-step classifiers tend to be complex and computationally intensive. The reason why their technique works so well is because the simple classifiers can be weak learners, which means that they don't need to be complex.

Consider the problem of building a table detector. We want to build a system that will automatically learn what a table looks like. Based on this knowledge, it should be able to identify whether there is a table in any given image. To build this system, the first step is to collect images that can be used to train our system. There are a lot of techniques available in the machine learning world that can be used to train a system like this. Keep in mind that we need to collect a lot of table and non-table images if we want our system to perform well. In machine learning lingo, table images are called **positive** samples and the non-table images are called **negative** samples. Our system will ingest this data and then learn to differentiate between these two classes.

In order to build a real-time system, we need to keep our classifier nice and simple. The only concern is that simple classifiers are not very accurate. If we try to make them more accurate, then they will end up being computationally intensive and hence slow. This kind of trade-off between accuracy and speed is very common in machine learning. So, we will overcome this problem by concatenating a bunch of weak classifiers to create a strong and unified classifier. We don't need the weak classifiers to be very accurate. To ensure the quality of the overall classifier, *Viola* and *Jones* have described a nifty technique in the cascading step. You can go through the paper to understand the complete system.

Now that we understand the general pipeline, let's see how to build a system that can detect faces in a live video. The first step is to extract features from all the images. In this case, the algorithms need these features to learn and understand what faces look like. They used Haar features in their paper to build the feature vectors. Once we extract these features, we pass them through a cascade of classifiers. We just check all the different rectangular subregions and keep discarding the ones that don't have faces in them. This way, we arrive at the final answer quickly to see whether a given rectangle contains a face or not.

What are integral images?

In order to extract these Haar features, we need to calculate the sum of the pixel values enclosed in many rectangular regions of the image. To make it scale invariant, we need to compute these areas at multiple scales (that is, for various rectangle sizes). If implemented naively, this would be a very computationally intensive process. We would have to iterate over all the pixels of each rectangle, including reading the same pixels multiple times if they are contained in different overlapping rectangles. If you want to build a system that can run in real time, you cannot spend so much time in computation. We need to find a way to avoid this huge redundancy during the area computation because we iterate over the same pixels multiple times. To avoid this, we can use something called **integral images**. These images can be initialized in a linear time (by iterating only twice over the image) and can then be provided with the sum of pixels inside any rectangle of any size by reading only four values. To understand it better, let's take a look at the following figure:

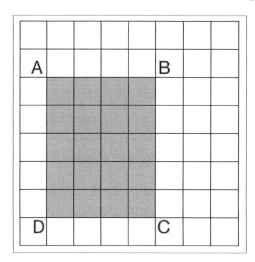

If we want to calculate the area of any rectangle in our image, we don't have to iterate through all the pixels in that region. Let's consider a rectangle formed by the top-left point in the image and any point P as the opposite corner. Let A_p denote the area of this rectangle. For example, in the preceding figure, A_B denotes the area of the 5 X 2 rectangle formed by taking the top-left point and B as opposite corners. Let's take a look at the following figure for clarity purposes:

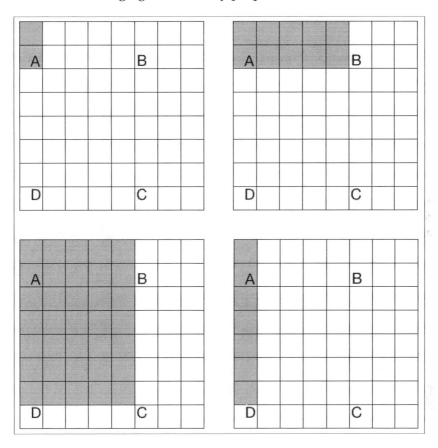

Let's take a look at the top-left diagram in the preceding figure. The colored pixels indicate the area between the top-left pixel and point A. This is denoted by A_A. The remaining diagrams are denoted by their respective names: A_B, A_C, and A_D. Now, if we want to calculate the area of the rectangle ABCD, as shown in the preceding figure, we will use the following formula:

Area of the rectangle ABCD = $A_C - (A_B + A_D - A_A)$

What's so special about this particular formula? As we know, extracting Haar features from the image includes computing these summations, and we would have to do it for a lot of rectangles at multiple scales in the image. A lot of these calculations are repetitive because we would be iterating over the same pixels over and over again. It is so slow that building a real-time system wouldn't be feasible. Hence, we need this formula. As you can see, we don't have to iterate over the same pixels multiple times. If we want to compute the area of any rectangle, all the values on the right-hand side of the previous equation are readily available in our integral image. We just use pick up the right values, substitute them in the previous equation, and extract the features.

Overlaying a facemask in a live video

OpenCV provides a nice face detection framework. We just need to load the cascade file and use it to detect the faces in an image. When we capture a video stream from the webcam, we can overlay funny masks on top of our faces. It will look something like this:

Let's take a look at the main parts of the code to see how to overlay the preceding mask on top of the face in the input video stream. The complete code is available in the downloadable code bundle provided along with this book:

```
int main(int argc, char* argv[])
{
    string faceCascadeName = argv[1];

    // Variable declarations and initializations

    // Iterate until the user presses the Esc key
    while(true)
    {
        // Capture the current frame
        cap >> frame;

        // Resize the frame
        resize(frame, frame, Size(), scalingFactor, scalingFactor,
            INTER_AREA);

        // Convert to grayscale
        cvtColor(frame, frameGray, CV_BGR2GRAY);

        // Equalize the histogram
        equalizeHist(frameGray, frameGray);

        // Detect faces
        faceCascade.detectMultiScale(frameGray, faces, 1.1, 2,
            0|CV_HAAR_SCALE_IMAGE, Size(30, 30) );
```

Let's see what happened here. We start reading input frames from the webcam and resize it to our size of choice. The captured frame is a color image and face detection works on grayscale images. So, we convert it to grayscale and equalize the histogram. Why do we need to equalize the histogram? We need to do this in order to compensate for any kind of issues, such as lighting, saturation, and so on. If the image is too bright or too dark, the detection will be poor. So, we need to equalize the histogram to ensure that our image has a healthy range of pixel values:

```
        // Draw green rectangle around the face
        for(int i = 0; i < faces.size(); i++)
        {
            Rect faceRect(faces[i].x, faces[i].y, faces[i].width,
                faces[i].height);
```

```
// Custom parameters to make the mask fit your face. You
may have to play around with them to make sure it works.
        int x = faces[i].x - int(0.1*faces[i].width);
        int y = faces[i].y - int(0.0*faces[i].height);
        int w = int(1.1 * faces[i].width);
        int h = int(1.3 * faces[i].height);

        // Extract region of interest (ROI) covering your face
        frameROI = frame(Rect(x,y,w,h));
```

At this point, we know where the face is. So, we extract the region of interest to overlay the mask in the right position:

```
        // Resize the face mask image based on the dimensions of
the above ROI
        resize(faceMask, faceMaskSmall, Size(w,h));

        // Convert the above image to grayscale
        cvtColor(faceMaskSmall, grayMaskSmall, CV_BGR2GRAY);

        // Threshold the above image to isolate the pixels
associated only with the face mask
        threshold(grayMaskSmall, grayMaskSmallThresh, 230, 255,
CV_THRESH_BINARY_INV);
```

We isolated the pixels associated with the face mask. Now, we want to overlay the mask in such a way that it doesn't look like a rectangle. We want the exact boundaries of the overlaid object so that it looks natural. Let's go ahead and overlay the mask now:

```
        // Create mask by inverting the above image (because we
don't want the background to affect the overlay)
        bitwise_not(grayMaskSmallThresh, grayMaskSmallThreshInv);

        // Use bitwise "AND" operator to extract precise boundary
of face mask
        bitwise_and(faceMaskSmall, faceMaskSmall, maskedFace,
grayMaskSmallThresh);

        // Use bitwise "AND" operator to overlay face mask
        bitwise_and(frameROI, frameROI, maskedFrame,
grayMaskSmallThreshInv);

        // Add the above masked images and place it in the
original frame ROI to create the final image
        add(maskedFace, maskedFrame, frame(Rect(x,y,w,h)));
```

```
    }

    // code dealing with memory release and GUi

    return 1;
}
```

What happened in the code?

The first thing to note is that this code takes two input arguments: the face cascade `xml` file and the mask image. You can use the `haarcascade_frontalface_alt.xml` and `facemask.jpg` files that are provided. We need a classifier model that can be used to detect faces in an image, and OpenCV provides a prebuilt xml file that can be used for this purpose. We use the `faceCascade.load()` function to load the `xml` file and also check whether the file has been loaded correctly.

We initiate the video capture object to capture the input frames from the webcam. We then convert it to grayscale to run the detector. The `detectMultiScale` function is used to extract the boundaries of all the faces in the input image. We may have to scale down the image according to our needs, so the second argument in this function takes care of this. This scaling factor is the jump that we take at each scale. Since we need to look for faces at multiple scales, the next size will be 1.1 times bigger than the current size. The last parameter is a threshold that specifies the number of adjacent rectangles that are needed to keep the current rectangle. It can be used to increase the robustness of the face detector.

We start the `while` loop and keep detecting the face in every frame until the user presses the *Esc* key. Once we detect a face, we need to overlay a mask on it. We may have to modify the dimensions slightly to ensure that the mask fits nicely. This customization is slightly subjective and it depends on the mask that's being used. Now that we have extracted the region of interest, we need to place our mask on top of this region. If we overlay the mask with its white background, it will look weird. We need to extract the exact curvy boundaries of the mask and overlay it. We want the skull-mask pixels to be visible and the remaining area to be transparent.

As we can see, the input mask has a white background. So, we create a mask by applying a threshold to the mask image. Using trial and error, we can see that a threshold of 240 works well. In the image, all the pixels with an intensity value greater than 240 will become 0, and all the others will become 255. As far as the region of interest is concerned in the image, we need to black out all the pixels in this region. To do this, we simply use the inverse of the mask that was just created. In the last step, we just add the masked versions to produce the final output image.

Get your sunglasses on

Now that we understand how to detect faces, we can generalize this concept to detect different parts of the face. We will use an eye detector to overlay sunglasses in a live video. It's important to understand that the Viola-Jones framework can be applied to any object. The accuracy and robustness will depend on the uniqueness of the object. For example, a human face has very unique characteristics, so it's easy to train our system to be robust. On the other hand, an object such as a towel is too generic, and there are no distinguishing characteristics as such. So, it's more difficult to build a robust towel detector.

Once you build the eye detector and overlay glasses on top of it, it will look something like this:

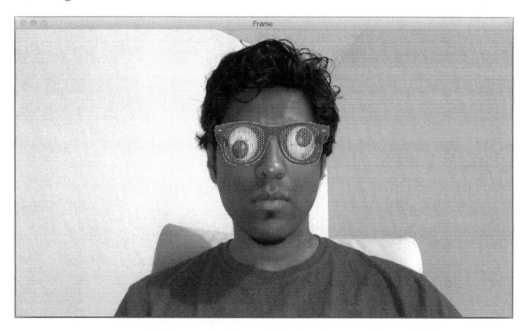

Let's take a look at the main parts of the code:

```
int main(int argc, char* argv[])
{
    string faceCascadeName = argv[1];
    string eyeCascadeName = argv[2];

    // Variable declarations and initializations

    // Face detection code
```

```
vector<Point> centers;

// Draw green circles around the eyes
for(int i = 0; i < faces.size(); i++)
{
    Mat faceROI = frameGray(faces[i]);
    vector<Rect> eyes;

    // In each face, detect eyes
    eyeCascade.detectMultiScale(faceROI, eyes, 1.1, 2, 0 |CV_
HAAR_SCALE_IMAGE, Size(30, 30));
```

As we can see here, we run the eye detector only in the face region. We don't need to search the entire image for eyes because we know that the eyes will always be on your face:

```
    // For each eye detected, compute the center
    for(int j = 0; j < eyes.size(); j++)
    {
        Point center( faces[i].x + eyes[j].x + int(eyes[j].
width*0.5), faces[i].y + eyes[j].y + int(eyes[j].height*0.5) );
        centers.push_back(center);
    }
}

// Overlay sunglasses only if both eyes are detected
if(centers.size() == 2)
{
    Point leftPoint, rightPoint;

    // Identify the left and right eyes
    if(centers[0].x < centers[1].x)
    {
        leftPoint = centers[0];
        rightPoint = centers[1];
    }
    else
    {
        leftPoint = centers[1];
        rightPoint = centers[0];
    }
```

We detect the eyes and store them only when we find both of them. We then use their coordinates to determine which one is the left eye and the right eye:

```
            // Custom parameters to make the sunglasses fit your face.
  You may have to play around with them to make sure it works.
            int w = 2.3 * (rightPoint.x - leftPoint.x);
            int h = int(0.4 * w);
            int x = leftPoint.x - 0.25*w;
            int y = leftPoint.y - 0.5*h;


            // Extract region of interest (ROI) covering both the eyes
            frameROI = frame(Rect(x,y,w,h));


            // Resize the sunglasses image based on the dimensions of
  the above ROI
            resize(eyeMask, eyeMaskSmall, Size(w,h));
```

In the preceding code, we adjusted the size of the sunglasses to fit the scale of our faces in the webcam:

```
            // Convert the above image to grayscale
            cvtColor(eyeMaskSmall, grayMaskSmall, CV_BGR2GRAY);


            // Threshold the above image to isolate the foreground
  object
            threshold(grayMaskSmall, grayMaskSmallThresh, 245, 255,
  CV_THRESH_BINARY_INV);


            // Create mask by inverting the above image (because we
  don't want the background to affect the overlay)
            bitwise_not(grayMaskSmallThresh, grayMaskSmallThreshInv);


            // Use bitwise "AND" operator to extract precise boundary
  of sunglasses
            bitwise_and(eyeMaskSmall, eyeMaskSmall, maskedEye,
  grayMaskSmallThresh);


            // Use bitwise "AND" operator to overlay sunglasses
            bitwise_and(frameROI, frameROI, maskedFrame,
  grayMaskSmallThreshInv);
```

```
            // Add the above masked images and place it in the
     original frame ROI to create the final image
            add(maskedEye, maskedFrame, frame(Rect(x,y,w,h)));
        }

        // code for memory release and GUI

    return 1;
}
```

Looking inside the code

If you notice, the flow of the code looks similar to the face detection code that we discussed earlier. We load the face detection cascade classifier as well as the eye detection cascade classifier. Now why do we need to load the face cascade classifier when we are detecting the eyes? Well, we don't really need to use the face detector, but it helps us limit our search for the eyes' location. We know that the eyes are always located on somebody's face, so we can limit the eye detection to the face region. The first step would be to detect the face and then run our eye detector code on this region. Since we would be operating on a smaller region, it would be faster and more efficient.

For each frame, we start by detecting the face. We then go ahead and detect the location of the eyes by operating on this region. After this step, we need to overlay the sunglasses. To do this, we need to resize the sunglasses' image to make sure that it fits our face. To get the proper scale, we can consider the distance between the two eyes that are being detected. We overlay the sunglasses only when we detect both the eyes. That's why we first run the eye detector, collect all the centers, and then overlay the sunglasses. Once we have this, we just need to overlay the sunglasses' mask. The principle used for masking is very similar to the principle that we used to overlay the facemask. You may have to customize the sizing and position of the sunglasses depending on what you want. You can play around with different types of sunglasses to see what they look like.

Tracking your nose, mouth, and ears

Now that you know how to track different things using the framework, you can try tracking your nose, mouth, and ears as well. Let's use a nose detector to overlay a funny nose on top:

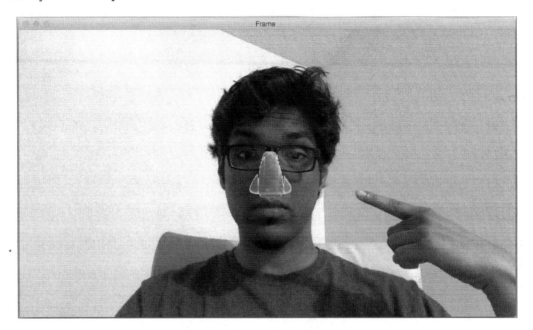

You can refer to the code files for a complete implementation of this detector. There are cascade files called `haarcascade_mcs_nose.xml`, `haarcascade_mcs_mouth.xml`, `haarcascade_mcs_leftear.xml`, and `haarcascade_mcs_rightear.xml` that can be used to track the different face parts. So, you can play around with them and try to overlay a moustache or Dracula ears on yourself!

Summary

In this chapter, we discussed Haar cascades and integral images. We learned how the face detection pipeline is built. We learned how to detect and track faces in a live video stream. We discussed how to use the face detection framework to detect various face parts, such as eyes, ears, nose, and mouth. We also learned how to overlay masks on top on the input image using the results of the face parts detection.

In the next chapter, we will learn about video surveillance, background removal, and morphological image processing.

8

Video Surveillance, Background Modeling, and Morphological Operations

In this chapter, we will learn how to detect a moving object in a video that is taken from a static camera. This is used extensively in video surveillance systems. We will discuss the different characteristics that can be used to build this system. We will learn about background modeling and see how we can use it to build a model of the background in a live video. Once we do this, we will combine all the blocks to detect the objects of interest in the video.

By the end of this chapter, you should be able to answer the following questions:

- What is naive background subtraction?
- What is frame differencing?
- How to build a background model?
- How to identify a new object in a static video?
- What is morphological image processing and how is it related to background modeling?
- How to achieve different effects using morphological operators?

Understanding background subtraction

Background subtraction is very useful in video surveillance. Basically, the background subtraction technique performs really well in cases where we need to detect moving objects in a static scene. Now, how is this useful for video surveillance? The process of video surveillance involves dealing with a constant data flow. The data stream keeps coming in at all times, and we need to analyze it to identify any suspicious activities. Let's consider the example of a hotel lobby. All the walls and furniture have a fixed location. Now, if we build a background model, we can use it to identify suspicious activities in the lobby. We can take advantage of the fact that the background scene remains static (which happens to be true in this case). This helps us avoid any unnecessary computation overheads.

As the name suggests, this algorithm works by detecting the background and assigning each pixel of an image to two classes: either the background (assuming that it's static and stable) or the foreground. It then subtracts the background from the current frame to obtain the foreground. By the static assumption, foreground objects will naturally correspond to objects or people moving in front of the background.

In order to detect moving objects, we first need to build a model of the background. This is not the same as direct frame differencing because we are actually modeling the background and using this model to detect moving objects. When we say that we are *modeling the background*, we are basically building a mathematical formulation that can be used to represent the background. So, this performs in a much better way than the simple frame differencing technique. This technique tries to detect static parts of the scene and then updates the background model. This background model is then used to detect background pixels. So, it's an adaptive technique that can adjust according to the scene.

Naive background subtraction

Let's start the background subtraction discussion from the beginning. What does a background subtraction process look like? Consider the following image:

The preceding image represents the background scene. Now, let's introduce a new object into this scene:

As shown in the preceding image, there is a new object in the scene. So, if we compute the difference between this image and our background model, you should be able to identify the location of the TV remote:

The overall process looks like this:

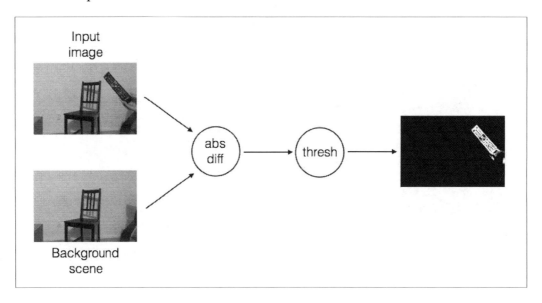

Does it work well?

There's a reason why we call it the **naive** approach. It works under ideal conditions, and as we know, nothing is ideal in the real world. It does a reasonably good job of computing the shape of the given object, but it does so under some constraints. One of the main requirements of this approach is that the color and intensity of the object should be sufficiently different from that of the background. Some of the factors that affect these kinds of algorithms are image noise, lighting conditions, autofocus in cameras, and so on.

Once a new object enters our scene and stays there, it will be difficult to detect new objects that are in front of it. This is because we don't update our background model, and the new object is now part of our background. Consider the following image:

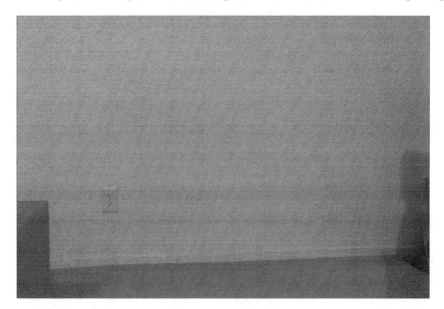

Now, let's say a new object enters our scene:

We identify this to be a new object, which is fine. Let's say another object comes into the scene:

It will be difficult to identify the location of these two different objects because their locations overlap. Here's what we get after subtracting the background and applying the threshold:

In this approach, we assume that the background is static. If some parts of our background start moving, then those parts will start getting detected as new objects. So, even if the movements are minor, say a waving flag, it will cause problems in our detection algorithm. This approach is also sensitive to changes in illumination, and it cannot handle any camera movement. Needless to say, it's a delicate approach! We need something that can handle all these things in the real world.

Frame differencing

We know that we cannot keep a static background image that can be used to detect objects. So, one of the ways to fix this would be to use frame differencing. It is one of the simplest techniques that we can use to see what parts of the video are moving. When we consider a live video stream, the difference between successive frames gives a lot of information. The concept is fairly straightforward. We just take the difference between successive frames and display the difference.

If I move my laptop rapidly, we can see something like this:

Instead of the laptop, let's move the object and see what happens. If I rapidly shake my head, it will look something like this:

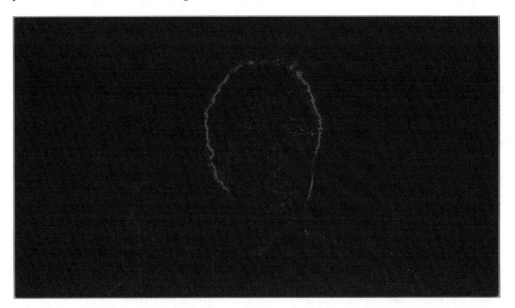

As you can see in the preceding images, only the moving parts of the video get highlighted. This gives us a good starting point to see the areas that are moving in the video. Let's take a look at the function to compute the frame difference:

```
Mat frameDiff(Mat prevFrame, Mat curFrame, Mat nextFrame)
{
    Mat diffFrames1, diffFrames2, output;

    // Compute absolute difference between current frame and the next
frame
    absdiff(nextFrame, curFrame, diffFrames1);

    // Compute absolute difference between current frame and the
previous frame
    absdiff(curFrame, prevFrame, diffFrames2);

    // Bitwise "AND" operation between the above two diff images
    bitwise_and(diffFrames1, diffFrames2, output);

    return output;
}
```

Frame differencing is fairly straightforward. You compute the absolute difference between the current frame and previous frame and between the current frame and next frame. We then take these frame differences and apply a bitwise AND operator. This will highlight the moving parts in the image. If you just compute the difference between the current frame and previous frame, it tends to be noisy. Hence, we need to use the bitwise AND operator between successive frame differences to get some stability when we see the moving objects.

Let's take a look at the function that can extract and return a frame from the webcam:

```
Mat getFrame(VideoCapture cap, float scalingFactor)
{
    //float scalingFactor = 0.5;
    Mat frame, output;

    // Capture the current frame
    cap >> frame;

    // Resize the frame
    resize(frame, frame, Size(), scalingFactor, scalingFactor, INTER_
AREA);
```

```
        // Convert to grayscale
        cvtColor(frame, output, CV_BGR2GRAY);

        return output;
}
```

As we can see, it's pretty straightforward. We just need to resize the frame and convert it to grayscale. Now that we have the helper functions ready, let's take a look at the `main` function and see how it all comes together:

```
int main(int argc, char* argv[])
{
    Mat frame, prevFrame, curFrame, nextFrame;
    char ch;

    // Create the capture object
    // 0 -> input arg that specifies it should take the input from the
webcam
    VideoCapture cap(0);

    // If you cannot open the webcam, stop the execution!
    if( !cap.isOpened() )
        return -1;

    //create GUI windows
    namedWindow("Frame");

    // Scaling factor to resize the input frames from the webcam
    float scalingFactor = 0.75;

    prevFrame = getFrame(cap, scalingFactor);
    curFrame = getFrame(cap, scalingFactor);
    nextFrame = getFrame(cap, scalingFactor);

    // Iterate until the user presses the Esc key
    while(true)
    {
        // Show the object movement
        imshow("Object Movement", frameDiff(prevFrame, curFrame,
nextFrame));

        // Update the variables and grab the next frame
        prevFrame = curFrame;
        curFrame = nextFrame;
        nextFrame = getFrame(cap, scalingFactor);

        // Get the keyboard input and check if it's 'Esc'
```

```
        // 27 -> ASCII value of 'Esc' key
        ch = waitKey( 30 );
        if (ch -- 27) {
            break;
        }
    }

    // Release the video capture object
    cap.release();

    // Close all windows
    destroyAllWindows();

    return 1;
}
```

How well does it work?

As we can see, frame differencing addresses a couple of important problems that we faced earlier. It can quickly adapt to lighting changes or camera movements. If an object comes in the frame and stays there, it will not be detected in the future frames. One of the main concerns of this approach is about detecting uniformly colored objects. It can only detect the edges of a uniformly colored object. This is because a large portion of this object will result in very low pixel differences, as shown in the following image:

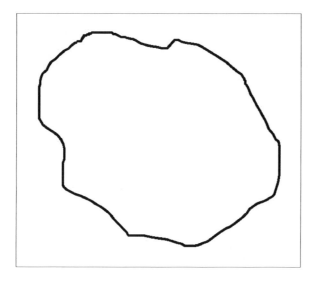

Let's say this object moved slightly. If we compare this with the previous frame, it will look like this:

Hence, we have very few pixels that are labeled on that object. Another concern is that it is difficult to detect whether an object is moving toward the camera or away from it.

The Mixture of Gaussians approach

Before we talk about **Mixture of Gaussians (MOG)**, let's see what a *mixture model* is. A mixture model is just a statistical model that can be used to represent the presence of subpopulations within our data. We don't really care about what category each data point belongs to. All we need to do is identify whether the data has multiple groups inside it. Now, if we represent each subpopulation using the Gaussian function, then it's called Mixture of Gaussians. Let's consider the following image:

Now, as we gather more frames in this scene, every part of the image will gradually become part of the background model. This is what we discussed earlier as well. If a scene is static, the model adapts itself to make sure that the background model is updated. The foreground mask, which is supposed to represent the foreground object, looks like a black image at this point because every pixel is part of the background model.

OpenCV has multiple algorithms implemented for the Mixture of Gaussians approach. One of them is called **MOG** and the other is called **MOG2**. To get a detailed explanation, you can refer to http://docs. opencv.org/master/db/d5c/tutorial_py_bg_subtraction. html#gsc.tab=0. You will also be able check out the original research papers that were used to implement these algorithms.

Let's introduce a new object into this scene and see what the foreground mask looks like using the MOG approach:

Let's wait for some time and introduce a new object into the scene. Let's take a look at what the new foreground mask looks like using the MOG2 approach:

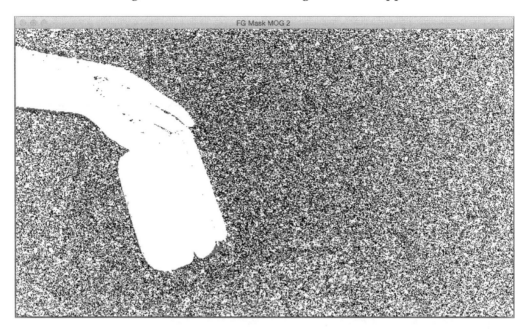

As you can see in the preceding images, the new objects are being identified correctly. Let's take a look at the interesting part of the code (you can get the complete code in the .cpp files):

```cpp
int main(int argc, char* argv[])
{
    // Variable declarations and initializations

    // Iterate until the user presses the Esc key
    while(true)
    {
        // Capture the current frame
        cap >> frame;

        // Resize the frame
        resize(frame, frame, Size(), scalingFactor, scalingFactor,
INTER_AREA);

        // Update the MOG background model based on the current frame
        pMOG->operator()(frame, fgMaskMOG);

        // Update the MOG2 background model based on the current frame
        pMOG2->operator()(frame, fgMaskMOG2);
```

```
        // Show the current frame
        //imshow("Frame", frame);

        // Show the MOG foreground mask
        imshow("FG Mask MOG", fgMaskMOG);

        // Show the MOG2 foreground mask
        imshow("FG Mask MOG 2", fgMaskMOG2);

        // Get the keyboard input and check if it's 'Esc'
        // 27 -> ASCII value of 'Esc' key
        ch = waitKey( 30 );
        if (ch == 27) {
            break;
        }
    }

    // Release the video capture object
    cap.release();

    // Close all windows
    destroyAllWindows();

    return 1;
}
```

What happened in the code?

Let's quickly go through the code and see what's happening there. We use the Mixture of Gaussians model to create a background subtractor object. This object represents the model that will be updated as and when we encounter new frames from the webcam. As we can see in the code, we initialize two background subtraction models: `BackgroundSubtractorMOG` and `BackgroundSubtractorMOG2`. They represent two different algorithms that are used for background subtraction. The first one refers to the paper by *P. KadewTraKuPong* and *R. Bowden titled, An improved adaptive background mixture model for real-time tracking with shadow detection*. You can check it out at `http://personal.ee.surrey.ac.uk/Personal/R.Bowden/publications/avbs01/avbs01.pdf`. The second one refers to the paper by *Z.Zivkovic* titled, *Improved adaptive Gausian Mixture Model for background subtraction*. You can check it out at `http://www.zoranz.net/Publications/zivkovic2004ICPR.pdf`. We start an infinite `while` loop and continuously read the input frames from the webcam. With each frame, we update the background model, as shown in the following lines:

```
pMOG->operator()(frame, fgMaskMOG);
pMOG2->operator()(frame, fgMaskMOG2);
```

The background model gets updated in these steps. Now, if a new object enters the scene and stays there, it will become part of the background model. This helps us overcome one of the biggest shortcomings of the naïve background subtraction model.

Morphological image processing

As discussed earlier, background subtraction methods are affected by many factors. Their accuracy depends on how we capture the data and how it's processed. One of the biggest factors that tend to affect these algorithms is the noise level. When we say *noise*, we are talking about things, such as graininess in an image, isolated black/white pixels, and so on. These issues tend to affect the quality of our algorithms. This is where morphological image processing comes into picture. Morphological image processing is used extensively in a lot of real-time systems to ensure the quality of the output.

Morphological image processing refers to processing the shapes of features in the image. For example, you can make a shape thicker or thinner. Morphological operators rely on how the pixels are ordered in an image, but on their values. This is the reason why they are really well suited to manipulate shapes in binary images. Morphological image processing can be applied to grayscale images as well, but the pixel values will not matter much.

What's the underlying principle?

Morphological operators use a structuring element to modify an image. What is a structuring element? A structuring element is basically a small shape that can be used to inspect a small region in the image. It is positioned at all the pixel locations in the image so that it can inspect that neighborhood. We basically take a small window and overlay it on top of a pixel. Depending on the response, we take an appropriate action at that pixel location.

Let's consider the following input image:

We will apply a bunch of morphological operations to this image to see how the shape changes.

Slimming the shapes

We can achieve this effect using an operation called **erosion**. This is an operation that makes a shape thinner by peeling the boundary layers of all the shapes in the image:

Let's take a look at the function that performs morphological erosion:

```
Mat performErosion(Mat inputImage, int erosionElement, int
erosionSize)
{
    Mat outputImage;
    int erosionType;

    if(erosionElement == 0)
        erosionType = MORPH_RECT;

    else if(erosionElement == 1)
        erosionType = MORPH_CROSS;

    else if(erosionElement == 2)
        erosionType = MORPH_ELLIPSE;

    // Create the structuring element for erosion
    Mat element = getStructuringElement(erosionType,
Size(2*erosionSize + 1, 2*erosionSize + 1), Point(erosionSize,
erosionSize));

    // Erode the image using the structuring element
    erode(inputImage, outputImage, element);

    // Return the output image
    return outputImage;
}
```

You can check out the complete code in the .cpp files to understand how to use this function. Basically, we build a structuring element using an built-in OpenCV function. This object is used as a probe to modify each pixel based on certain conditions. These *conditions* refer to what's happening around that particular pixel in the image. For example, is it surrounded by white pixels? Or is it surrounded by black pixels? Once we have an answer, we can take an appropriate action.

Thickening the shapes

We use an operation called **dilation** to achieve thickening. This is an operation that makes a shape thicker by adding boundary layers to all the shapes in the image:

Here is the code to do this:

```cpp
Mat performDilation(Mat inputImage, int dilationElement, int
dilationSize)
{
    Mat outputImage;
    int dilationType;

    if(dilationElement == 0)
        dilationType = MORPH_RECT;

    else if(dilationElement == 1)
        dilationType = MORPH_CROSS;

    else if(dilationElement == 2)
        dilationType = MORPH_ELLIPSE;

    // Create the structuring element for dilation
    Mat element = getStructuringElement(dilationType,
Size(2*dilationSize + 1, 2*dilationSize + 1), Point(dilationSize,
dilationSize));
```

```
    // Dilate the image using the structuring element
    dilate(inputImage, outputImage, element);

    // Return the output image
    return outputImage;
}
```

Other morphological operators

Here are some other morphological operators that are interesting. Let's first take a look at the output image. We can take a look at the code at the end of this section.

Morphological opening

This is an operation that *opens* a shape. This operator is frequently used for noise removal in an image. We can achieve morphological opening by applying erosion followed by dilation to an image. The morphological opening process basically removes small objects from the foreground in the image by placing them in the background:

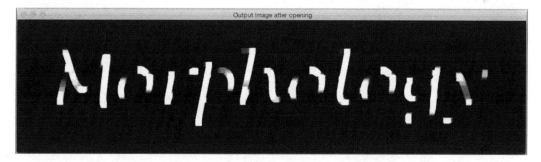

Here is the function to the perform morphological opening:

```
Mat performOpening(Mat inputImage, int morphologyElement, int
morphologySize)
{
    Mat outputImage, tempImage;
    int morphologyType;

    if(morphologyElement == 0)
        morphologyType = MORPH_RECT;

    else if(morphologyElement == 1)
        morphologyType = MORPH_CROSS;
```

```
      else if(morphologyElement == 2)
          morphologyType = MORPH_ELLIPSE;

      // Create the structuring element for erosion
      Mat element = getStructuringElement(morphologyTy
pe, Size(2*morphologySize + 1, 2*morphologySize + 1),
Point(morphologySize, morphologySize));

      // Apply morphological opening to the image using the structuring
element
      erode(inputImage, tempImage, element);
      dilate(tempImage, outputImage, element);

      // Return the output image
      return outputImage;
}
```

As we can see here, we apply erosion and dilation to the image to perform the morphological opening.

Morphological closing

This is an operation that *closes* a shape by filling the gaps. This operation is also used for noise removal. We achieve morphological closing by applying dilation followed by erosion to an image. This operation removes tiny holes in the foreground by changing small objects in the background into the foreground.

Let's quickly take a look at the function to perform the morphological closing:

```
Mat performClosing(Mat inputImage, int morphologyElement, int
morphologySize)
{
    Mat outputImage, tempImage;
    int morphologyType;
```

```
    if(morphologyElement == 0)
        morphologyType = MORPH_RECT;

    else if(morphologyElement == 1)
        morphologyType = MORPH_CROSS;

    else if(morphologyElement == 2)
        morphologyType = MORPH_ELLIPSE;

    // Create the structuring element for erosion
    Mat element = getStructuringElement(morphologyTy
pe, Size(2*morphologySize + 1, 2*morphologySize + 1),
Point(morphologySize, morphologySize));

    // Apply morphological opening to the image using the structuring
element
    dilate(inputImage, tempImage, element);
    erode(tempImage, outputImage, element);

    // Return the output image
    return outputImage;
}
```

Drawing the boundary

We achieve this using the morphological gradient. This is an operation that draws
the boundary around a shape by taking the difference between dilation and erosion
of an image:

Let's take a look at the function to perform the morphological gradient:

```
Mat performMorphologicalGradient(Mat inputImage, int
morphologyElement, int morphologySize)
{
    Mat outputImage, tempImage1, tempImage2;
    int morphologyType;

    if(morphologyElement == 0)
        morphologyType = MORPH_RECT;

    else if(morphologyElement == 1)
        morphologyType = MORPH_CROSS;

    else if(morphologyElement == 2)
        morphologyType = MORPH_ELLIPSE;

    // Create the structuring element for erosion
    Mat element = getStructuringElement(morphologyTy
pe, Size(2*morphologySize + 1, 2*morphologySize + 1),
Point(morphologySize, morphologySize));

    // Apply morphological gradient to the image using the structuring
element
    dilate(inputImage, tempImage1, element);
    erode(inputImage, tempImage2, element);

    // Return the output image
    return tempImage1 - tempImage2;
}
```

White Top-Hat transform

While Top-Hat transform, also simply called Top-Hat transform, extracts finer details from the images. We can apply white top-hat transform by computing the difference between the input image and its morphological opening. This gives us the objects in the image that are smaller than the structuring elements and are brighter than the surroundings. So, depending on the size of the structuring element, we can extract various objects in the given image:

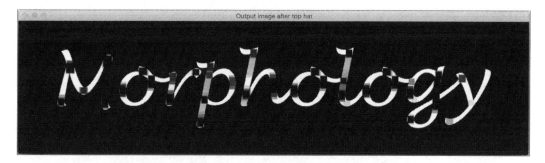

If you look carefully at the output image, you can see those black rectangles. This means that the structuring element was able to fit in there, and so those regions are blackened out. Here is the function to do this:

```
Mat performTopHat(Mat inputImage, int morphologyElement, int
morphologySize)
{
    Mat outputImage;
    int morphologyType;

    if(morphologyElement == 0)
        morphologyType = MORPH_RECT;

    else if(morphologyElement == 1)
        morphologyType = MORPH_CROSS;

    else if(morphologyElement == 2)
        morphologyType = MORPH_ELLIPSE;

    // Create the structuring element for erosion
    Mat element = getStructuringElement(morphologyTy
pe, Size(2*morphologySize + 1, 2*morphologySize + 1),
Point(morphologySize, morphologySize));

    // Apply top hat operation to the image using the structuring
element
    outputImage = inputImage - performOpening(inputImage,
morphologyElement, morphologySize);

    // Return the output image
    return outputImage;
}
```

Black Top-Hat transform

Black Top-Hat transform, also simply called Black Hat transform, extracts finer details from the image as well. We can apply black top-hat transform by computing the difference between the morphological closing of an image and the image itself. This gives us the objects in the image that are smaller than the structuring element and are darker than the surroundings.

Let's take a look at the function to perform the black hat transform:

```cpp
Mat performBlackHat(Mat inputImage, int morphologyElement, int morphologySize)
{
    Mat outputImage;
    int morphologyType;

    if(morphologyElement == 0)
        morphologyType = MORPH_RECT;

    else if(morphologyElement == 1)
        morphologyType = MORPH_CROSS;

    else if(morphologyElement == 2)
        morphologyType = MORPH_ELLIPSE;

    // Create the structuring element for erosion
    Mat element = getStructuringElement(morphologyType, Size(2*morphologySize + 1, 2*morphologySize + 1),
Point(morphologySize, morphologySize));

    // Apply black hat operation to the image using the structuring element
    outputImage = performClosing(inputImage, morphologyElement, morphologySize) - inputImage;

    // Return the output image
    return outputImage;
}
```

Summary

In this chapter, we learned about the algorithms that are used for background modeling and morphological image processing. We discussed naïve background subtraction and its limitations. We learned how to get motion information using frame differencing and how it can be constrain us when we want to track different types of objects. We also discussed Mixture of Gaussians, along with its formulation and implementation details. We then discussed morphological image processing. We learned how it can be used for various purposes and different operations were demonstrated to show the use cases.

In the next chapter, we will discuss how to track an object and the various techniques that can be used to do it.

9
Learning Object Tracking

In the previous chapter, we learned about video surveillance, background modeling, and morphological image processing. We discussed how we can use different morphological operators to apply cool visual effects to input images. In this chapter, we will learn how to track an object in a live video. We will discuss the different characteristics of an object that can be used to track it. We will also learn about different methods and techniques used for object tracking. Object tracking is used extensively in robotics, self-driving cars, vehicle tracking, player tracking in sports, video compression, and so on.

By the end of this chapter, you will learn:

- How to track colored objects
- How to build an interactive object tracker
- What is a corner detector
- How to detect good features to track
- How to build an optical flow-based feature tracker

Tracking objects of a specific color

In order to build a good object tracker, we need to understand what characteristics can be used to make our tracking robust and accurate. So, let's take a baby step in this direction, and see how we can use colorspaces to come up with a good visual tracker. One thing to keep in mind is that the color information is sensitive to lighting conditions. In real-world applications, you need to do some preprocessing to take care of this. But for now, let's assume that somebody else is doing this and we are getting clean color images.

There are many different colorspaces and picking up a good one will depend on what people use for different applications. While RGB is the native representation on the computer screen, it's not necessarily ideal for humans. When it comes to humans, we give names to colors that are based on their hue. This is why **HSV (Hue Saturation Value)** is probably one of the most informative colorspaces. It closely aligns with how we perceive colors. Hue refers to the color spectrum, saturation refers to the intensity of a particular color, and value refers to the brightness of that pixel. This is actually represented in a cylindrical format. You can refer to a simple explanation about this at `http://infohost.nmt.edu/tcc/help/pubs/colortheory/web/hsv.html`. We can take the pixels of an image to the HSV space and then use colorspace distances and threshold in this space thresholding to track a given object.

Consider the following frame in the video:

If you run it through the colorspace filter and track the object, you will see something like this:

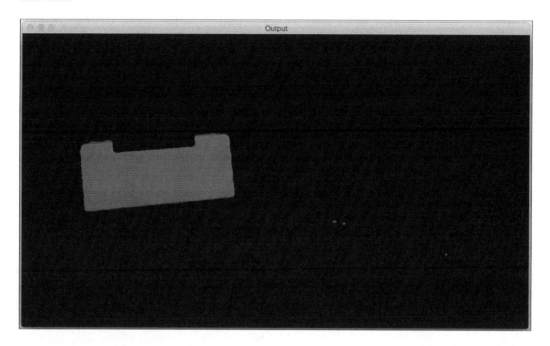

As you can see here, our tracker recognizes a particular object in the video based on its color characteristics. In order to use this tracker, we need to know the color distribution of our target object. The following code is used to track a colored object that selects only pixels that have a certain given hue. The code is well commented, so read the explanation mentioned previously for each line to see what's happening:

```
int main(int argc, char* argv[])
{
    // Variable declarations and initializations

    // Iterate until the user presses the Esc key
    while(true)
    {
        // Initialize the output image before each iteration
        outputImage = Scalar(0,0,0);

        // Capture the current frame
        cap >> frame;
```

```
        // Check if 'frame' is empty
        if(frame.empty())
            break;

        // Resize the frame
        resize(frame, frame, Size(), scalingFactor, scalingFactor,
          INTER_AREA);
        // Convert to HSV colorspace
        cvtColor(frame, hsvImage, COLOR_BGR2HSV);

        // Define the range of "blue" color in HSV colorspace
        Scalar lowerLimit = Scalar(60,100,100);
        Scalar upperLimit = Scalar(180,255,255);

        // Threshold the HSV image to get only blue color
        inRange(hsvImage, lowerLimit, upperLimit, mask);

        // Compute bitwise-AND of input image and mask
        bitwise_and(frame, frame, outputImage, mask=mask);

        // Run median filter on the output to smoothen it
        medianBlur(outputImage, outputImage, 5);

        // Display the input and output image
        imshow("Input", frame);
        imshow("Output", outputImage);

        // Get the keyboard input and check if it's 'Esc'
        // 30 -> wait for 30 ms
        // 27 -> ASCII value of 'ESC' key
        ch = waitKey(30);
        if (ch == 27) {
            break;
        }
    }

    return 1;
}
```

Building an interactive object tracker

A colorspace-based tracker gives us the freedom to track a colored object, but we are also constrained to a predefined color. What if we just want to randomly pick an object? How do we build an object tracker that can learn the characteristics of the selected object and track it automatically? This is where the CAMShift algorithm, which stands for **Continuously Adaptive Meanshift**, comes into the picture. It's basically an improved version of the Meanshift algorithm.

The concept of Meanshift is actually nice and simple. Let's say we select a region of interest, and we want our object tracker to track that object. In this region, we select a bunch of points based on the color histogram and compute the centroid of spatial points. If the centroid lies at the center of this region, we know that the object hasn't moved. But if the centroid is not at the center of this region, then we know that the object is moving in some direction. The movement of the centroid controls the direction in which the object is moving. So, we move the bounding box of the object to a new location so that the new centroid becomes the center of this bounding box. Hence, this algorithm is called Meanshift because the mean (that is, the centroid) is shifting. This way, we keep ourselves updated with the current location of the object.

However, the problem with Meanshift is that the size of the bounding box is not allowed to change. When you move the object away from the camera, the object will appear smaller to the human eye, but Meanshift will not take this into account. The size of the bounding box will remain the same throughout the tracking session. Hence, we need to use CAMShift. The advantage of CAMShift is that it can adapt the size of the bounding box to the size of the object. Along with this, it can also keep track of the orientation of the object.

Let's consider the following figure in which the object is highlighted:

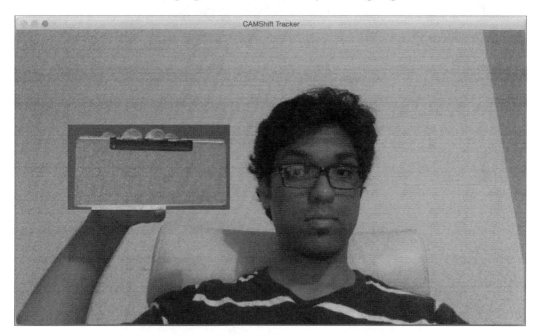

Now that we have selected the object, the algorithm computes the histogram backprojection and extracts all the information. What is histogram backprojection? It's just a way of identifying how well the image fits into our histogram model. We compute the histogram model of a particular thing, and then use this model to find that thing in an image. Let's move the object and see how it gets tracked:

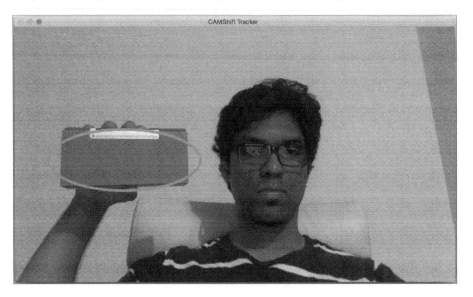

Looks like the object is getting tracked fairly well. Let's change the orientation, and check whether the tracking is maintained:

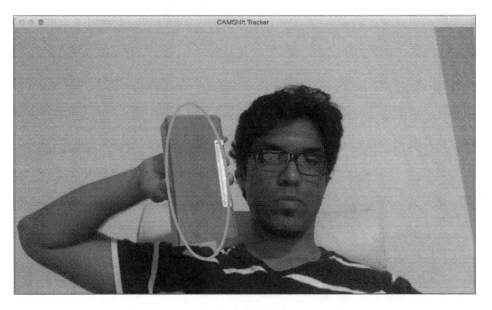

As you can see, the bounding ellipse has changed its location as well as its orientation. Let's change the perspective of the object, and see whether it's still able to track it:

We are still good! The bounding ellipse has changed the aspect ratio to reflect the fact that the object looks skewed now (because of the perspective transformation). Let's take a look at the user interface functionality in the following code:

```cpp
Mat image;
Point originPoint;
Rect selectedRect;
bool selectRegion = false;
int trackingFlag = 0;

// Function to track the mouse events
void onMouse(int event, int x, int y, int, void*)
{
    if(selectRegion)
    {
        selectedRect.x = MIN(x, originPoint.x);
        selectedRect.y = MIN(y, originPoint.y);
        selectedRect.width = std::abs(x - originPoint.x);
        selectedRect.height = std::abs(y - originPoint.y);
```

```
            selectedRect &= Rect(0, 0, image.cols, image.rows);
    }

    switch(event)
    {
        case CV_EVENT_LBUTTONDOWN:
            originPoint = Point(x,y);
            selectedRect = Rect(x,y,0,0);
            selectRegion = true;
            break;

        case CV_EVENT_LBUTTONUP:
            selectRegion = false;
            if( selectedRect.width > 0 && selectedRect.height > 0 )
            {
                trackingFlag = -1;
            }
            break;
    }
}
```

This function basically captures the coordinates of the rectangle that were selected in the window. The user just needs to click on them and drag them with the mouse. There are a set of inbuilt functions in OpenCV that help us detect these different mouse events.

Here is the code used to perform object tracking based on CAMShift:

```
int main(int argc, char* argv[])
{
    // Variable declaration and initialization

    // Iterate until the user presses the Esc key
    while(true)
    {
        // Capture the current frame
        cap >> frame;

        // Check if 'frame' is empty
        if(frame.empty())
            break;
```

```
    // Resize the frame
    resize(frame, frame, Size(), scalingFactor, scalingFactor,
       INTER_AREA);

    // Clone the input frame
    frame.copyTo(image);

    // Convert to HSV colorspace
    cvtColor(image, hsvImage, COLOR_BGR2HSV);
```

We now have the HSV image waiting to be processed at this point. Let's go ahead and see how we can use our thresholds to process this image:

```
    if(trackingFlag)
    {
        // Check for all the values in 'hsvimage' that are
        within the specified range
        // and put the result in 'mask'
        inRange(hsvImage, Scalar(0, minSaturation, minValue),
          Scalar(180, 256, maxValue), mask);

        // Mix the specified channels
        int channels[] = {0, 0};
         hueImage.create(hsvImage.size(), hsvImage.depth());
        mixChannels(&hsvImage, 1, &hueImage, 1, channels, 1);

        if(trackingFlag < 0)
        {
        // Create images based on selected regions of interest
            Mat roi(hueImage, selectedRect), maskroi(mask,
               selectedRect);

            // Compute the histogram and normalize it
             calcHist(&roi, 1, 0, maskroi, hist, 1, &histSize,
               &histRanges);
            normalize(hist, hist, 0, 255, CV_MINMAX);

            trackingRect = selectedRect;
            trackingFlag = 1;
        }
```

As you can see here, we use the HSV image to compute the histogram of the region. We use our thresholds to locate the required color in the HSV spectrum and then filter out the image based on that. Let's go ahead and see how we can compute the histogram backprojection:

```
// Compute the histogram backprojection
calcBackProject(&hueImage, 1, 0, hist, backproj,
    &histRanges);
backproj &= mask;
RotatedRect rotatedTrackingRect = CamShift(backproj,
    trackingRect, TermCriteria(CV_TERMCRIT_EPS |
        CV_TERMCRIT_ITER, 10, 1));

// Check if the area of trackingRect is too small
if(trackingRect.area() <= 1)
{
    // Use an offset value to make sure the
trackingRect has a minimum size
    int cols = backproj.cols, rows = backproj.rows;
    int offset = MIN(rows, cols) + 1;
    trackingRect = Rect(trackingRect.x - offset,
    trackingRect.y - offset, trackingRect.x + offset,
    trackingRect.y + offset) & Rect(0, 0, cols, rows);
}
```

We are now ready to display the results. Using the rotated rectangle, let's draw an ellipse around our region of interest:

```
// Draw the ellipse on top of the image
ellipse(image, rotatedTrackingRect, Scalar(0,255,0), 3,
CV_AA);
}


// Apply the 'negative' effect on the selected region of
interest
if(selectRegion && selectedRect.width > 0 && selectedRect.
height > 0)
{
    Mat roi(image, selectedRect);
    bitwise_not(roi, roi);
}

// Display the output image
imshow(windowName, image);
```

```
    // Get the keyboard input and check if it's 'Esc'
    // 27 -> ASCII value of 'Esc' key
    ch = waitKey(30);
    if (ch == 27) {
        break;
    }
}

return 1;
}
```

Detecting points using the Harris corner detector

Corner detection is a technique used to detect *interest points* in the image. These interest points are also called *feature points* or simply *features* in Computer Vision terminology. A corner is basically an intersection of two edges. An *interest point* is basically something that can be uniquely detected in an image. A corner is a particular case of an interest point. These interest points help us characterize an image. These points are used extensively in applications, such as object tracking, image classification, visual search, and so on. Since we know that the corners are *interesting*, let's see how we can detect them.

In Computer Vision, there is a popular corner detection technique called the Harris corner detector. We construct a 2 x 2 matrix based on partial derivatives of the grayscale image, and then analyze the eigenvalues. Now what does this mean? Well, let's dissect it so that we can understand it better. Let's consider a small patch in the image. Our goal is to check whether this patch has a corner in it. So, we consider all the neighboring patches and compute the intensity difference between our patch and all those neighboring patches. If the difference is high in all directions, then we know that our patch has a corner in it. This is actually an oversimplification of the actual algorithm, but it covers the gist. If you want to understand the underlying mathematical details, you can take a look at the original paper by Harris and Stephens at http://www.bmva.org/bmvc/1988/avc-88-023.pdf. A corner point is a point where both the eigenvalues would have large values.

If we run the Harris corner detector, it will look like this:

As you can see, the green circles on the TV remote are the detected corners. This will change based on the parameters you choose for the detector. If you modify the parameters, you can see that more points might get detected. If you make it strict, then you might not be able to detect soft corners. Let's take a look at the following code to detect Harris corners:

```
int main(int argc, char* argv[])
{
    // Variable declaration and initialization

    // Iterate until the user presses the Esc key
    while(true)
    {
        // Capture the current frame
        cap >> frame;

        // Resize the frame
        resize(frame, frame, Size(), scalingFactor, scalingFactor,
            INTER_AREA);

        dst = Mat::zeros(frame.size(), CV_32FC1);
```

```
// Convert to grayscale
cvtColor(frame, frameGray, COLOR_BGR2GRAY );

// Detecting corners
cornerHarris(frameGray, dst, blockSize, apertureSize, k,
  BORDER_DEFAULT);

// Normalizing
normalize(dst, dst_norm, 0, 255, NORM_MINMAX, CV_32FC1,
  Mat());
convertScaleAbs(dst_norm, dst_norm_scaled);
```

We converted the image to grayscale and detected corners using our parameters. You can find the complete code in the `.cpp` files. These parameters play an important role in the number of points that will be detected. You can check out the OpenCV documentation of the Harris corner detector at `http://docs.opencv.org/2.4/ modules/imgproc/doc/feature_detection.html?highlight=cornerharris#v oid cornerHarris(InputArray src, OutputArray dst, int blockSize, int ksize, double k, int borderType)`.

We now have all the information that we need. Let's go ahead and draw circles around our corners to display the results:

```
// Drawing a circle around each corner
for(int j = 0; j < dst_norm.rows ; j++)
{
    for(int i = 0; i < dst_norm.cols; i++)
    {
        if((int)dst_norm.at<float>(j,i) > thresh)
        {
            circle(frame, Point(i, j), 8,  Scalar(0,255,0), 2,
8, 0);
        }
    }
}

// Showing the result
imshow(windowName, frame);

// Get the keyboard input and check if it's 'Esc'
// 27 -> ASCII value of 'Esc' key
ch = waitKey(10);
if (ch == 27) {
    break;
}
}

// Release the video capture object
```

```
        cap.release();

        // Close all windows
        destroyAllWindows();

        return 1;
}
```

As you can see, this code takes a `blockSize` input argument. Depending on the size you choose, the performance will vary. Start with a value of 4 and play around with it to see what happens.

Shi-Tomasi Corner Detector

The Harris corner detector performs well in many cases, but it can still be improved. Around six years after the original paper by Harris and Stephens, Shi-Tomasi came up with something better and they called it *Good Features To Track*. You can read the original paper at: `http://www.ai.mit.edu/courses/6.891/handouts/shi94good.pdf`. They used a different scoring function to improve the overall quality. Using this method, we can find the N strongest corners in the given image. This is very useful when we don't want to use every single corner to extract information from the image. As discussed earlier, a good interest point detector is very useful in applications, such as object tracking, object recognition, image search, and so on.

If you apply the Shi-Tomasi corner detector to an image, you will see something like this:

As you can see here, all the important points in the frame are captured. Let's take a look at the following code to track these features:

```cpp
int main(int argc, char* argv[])
{
    // Variable declaration and initialization

    // Iterate until the user presses the Esc key
    while(true)
    {
        // Capture the current frame
        cap >> frame;

        // Resize the frame
        resize(frame, frame, Size(), scalingFactor, scalingFactor,
            INTER_AREA);

        // Convert to grayscale
        cvtColor(frame, frameGray, COLOR_BGR2GRAY );

        // Initialize the parameters for Shi-Tomasi algorithm
        vector<Point2f> corners;
        double qualityThreshold = 0.02;
        double minDist = 15;
        int blockSize = 5;
        bool useHarrisDetector = false;
        double k = 0.07;

        // Clone the input frame
        Mat frameCopy;
        frameCopy = frame.clone();

        // Apply corner detection
        goodFeaturesToTrack(frameGray, corners, numCorners,
            qualityThreshold, minDist, Mat(), blockSize,
            useHarrisDetector, k);
```

We extracted the frame and used `goodFeaturesToTrack` to detect the corners. It's important to understand that the number of corners detected will depend on our choice of parameters. You can find a detailed explanation at http://docs.opencv.org/2.4/modules/imgproc/doc/feature_detection.html?highlight=goodfeaturestotrack#goodfeaturestotrack. Let's go ahead and draw circles on these points to display the output image:

```cpp
        // Parameters for the circles to display the corners
        int radius = 8;        // radius of the cirles
        int thickness = 2;     // thickness of the circles
        int lineType = 8;
```

```
// Draw the detected corners using circles
for(size_t i = 0; i < corners.size(); i++)
{
    Scalar color = Scalar(rng.uniform(0,255),
        rng.uniform(0,255), rng.uniform(0,255));
    circle(frameCopy, corners[i], radius, color,
        thickness, lineType, 0);
}

/// Show what you got
imshow(windowName, frameCopy);

// Get the keyboard input and check if it's 'Esc'
// 27 -> ASCII value of 'Esc' key
ch = waitKey(30);
if (ch == 27) {
    break;
}
}

// Release the video capture object
cap.release();

// Close all windows
destroyAllWindows();

return 1;
}
```

This program takes a `numCorners` input argument. This value indicates the maximum number of corners you want to track. Start with a value of `100` and play around with it to see what happens. If you increase this value, you will see more feature points getting detected.

Feature-based tracking

Feature-based tracking refers to tracking individual feature points across successive frames in the video. The advantage here is that we don't have to detect feature points in every single frame. We can just detect them once and keep tracking them after that. This is more efficient as compared to running the detector on every frame. We use a technique called optical flow to track these features. Optical flow is one of the most popular techniques in Computer Vision. We choose a bunch of feature points, and track them through the video stream. When we detect the feature points, we compute the displacement vectors and show the motion of those keypoints between consecutive frames. These vectors are called motion vectors.

A motion vector for a particular point is just a directional line that indicates where that point has moved as compared to the previous frame. Different methods are used to detect these motion vectors. The two most popular algorithms are the Lucas-Kanade method and Farneback algorithm.

The Lucas-Kanade method

The Lucas-Kanade method is used for sparse optical flow tracking. By sparse, we mean that the number of feature points is relatively low. You can refer to their original paper at `http://cseweb.ucsd.edu/classes/sp02/cse252/lucaskanade81.pdf`. We start the process by extracting the feature points. For each feature point, we create 3 x 3 patches with the feature point at the center. We assume that all the points within each patch will have a similar motion. We can adjust the size of this window, depending on the problem at hand.

For each feature point in the current frame, we take the surrounding 3 x 3 patch as our reference point. For this patch, we take a look at its neighborhood in the previous frame to get the best match. This neighborhood is usually bigger than 3 x 3 because we want to get the patch that's closest to the patch under consideration. Now, the path from the center pixel of the matched patch in the previous frame to the center pixel of the patch under consideration in the current frame will become the motion vector. We do this for all the feature points, and extract all the motion vectors.

Let's consider the following frame:

We need to add some points that we want to track. Just go ahead and click on a bunch of points on this window with your mouse:

If I move to a different position, you will see that the points are still being tracked correctly within a small margin of error:

Let's add a lot of points and see what happens:

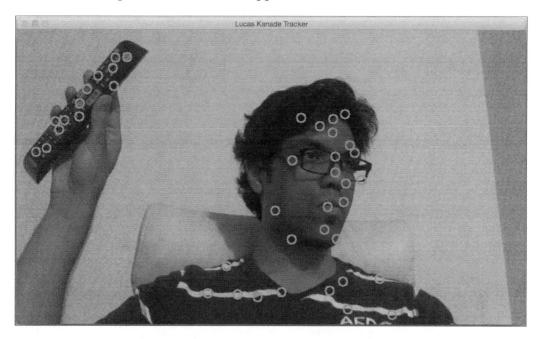

As you can see, it will keep tracking those points. However, you will notice that some of the points will be dropped in between because of factors, such as prominence, speed of the movement, and so on. If you want to play around with it, you can just keep adding more points to it. You can also allow the user to select a region of interest in the input video. You can then extract feature points from this region of interest and track the object by drawing the bounding box. It will be a fun exercise!

Here is the code used to perform Lucas-Kanade-based tracking:

```
int main(int argc, char* argv[])
{
    // Variable declaration and initialization

    // Iterate until the user hits the Esc key
    while(true)
    {
        // Capture the current frame
        cap >> frame;

        // Check if the frame is empty
        if(frame.empty())
```

```
        break;

        // Resize the frame
        resize(frame, frame, Size(), scalingFactor, scalingFactor,
INTER_AREA);

        // Copy the input frame
        frame.copyTo(image);

        // Convert the image to grayscale
        cvtColor(image, curGrayImage, COLOR_BGR2GRAY);

        // Check if there are points to track
        if(!trackingPoints[0].empty())
        {
            // Status vector to indicate whether the flow for the
corresponding features has been found
            vector<uchar> statusVector;

            // Error vector to indicate the error for the
corresponding feature
            vector<float> errorVector;

            // Check if previous image is empty
            if(prevGrayImage.empty())
            {
                curGrayImage.copyTo(prevGrayImage);
            }

            // Calculate the optical flow using Lucas-Kanade algorithm
            calcOpticalFlowPyrLK(prevGrayImage, curGrayImage,
trackingPoints[0], trackingPoints[1], statusVector, errorVector,
windowSize, 3, terminationCriteria, 0, 0.001);
```

We use the current image and the previous image to compute the optical flow information. Needless to say that the quality of the output will depend on the parameters you have chosen. You can find more details about the parameters at http://docs.opencv.org/2.4/modules/video/doc/motion_analysis_and_object_tracking.html#calcopticalflowpyrlk. To increase the quality and robustness, we need to filter out the points that are very close to each other because they do not add the new information. Let's go ahead and do that:

```
        int count = 0;

        // Minimum distance between any two tracking points
        int minDist = 7;
```

```
            for(int i=0; i < trackingPoints[1].size(); i++)
            {
                if(pointTrackingFlag)
                {
                    /* If the new point is within 'minDist' distance
from an existing point, it will not be tracked */
                    if(norm(currentPoint - trackingPoints[1][i]) <=
minDist)
                    {
                        pointTrackingFlag = false;
                        continue;
                    }
                }

                // Check if the status vector is good
                if(!statusVector[i])
                    continue;

                trackingPoints[1][count++] = trackingPoints[1][i];

        // Draw a filled circle for each of the tracking points
                int radius = 8;
                int thickness = 2;
                int lineType = 8;
                circle(image, trackingPoints[1][i], radius,
                    Scalar(0,255,0), thickness, lineType);
            }

            trackingPoints[1].resize(count);
    }
```

We now have the tracking points. The next step is to refine the location of these points. What exactly does "refine" mean in this context? To increase the speed of computation, there is some level of quantization involved. In layman's terms, you can think of it as "rounding off". Now that we have the approximate region, we can refine the location of the point within that region to get a more accurate outcome. Let's go ahead and do this:

```
            // Refining the location of the feature points
            if(pointTrackingFlag && trackingPoints[1].size() <
              maxNumPoints)
            {
                vector<Point2f> tempPoints;
                tempPoints.push_back(currentPoint);

                // Function to refine the location of the corners to
subpixel accuracy.
```

```
        // Here, 'pixel' refers to the image patch of size
  'windowSize' and not the actual image pixel
            cornerSubPix(curGrayImage, tempPoints, windowSize,
  cvSize(-1,-1), terminationCriteria);

            trackingPoints[1].push_back(tempPoints[0]);
            pointTrackingFlag = false;
        }

        // Display the image with the tracking points
        imshow(windowName, image);

        // Check if the user pressed the Esc key
        char ch = waitKey(10);
        if(ch == 27)
            break;

        // Swap the 'points' vectors to update 'previous' to
          'current'
        std::swap(trackingPoints[1], trackingPoints[0]);

        // Swap the images to update previous image to current image
        cv::swap(prevGrayImage, curGrayImage);
    }

    return 1;
}
```

The Farneback algorithm

Gunnar Farneback proposed this optical flow algorithm and it's used for dense
tracking. Dense tracking is used extensively in robotics, augmented reality, 3D
mapping, and so on. You can check out the original paper at http://www.diva-
portal.org/smash/get/diva2:273847/FULLTEXT01.pdf. The Lucas-Kanade
method is a sparse technique, which means that we only need to process some pixels
in the entire image. The Farneback algorithm, on the other hand, is a dense technique
that requires us to process all the pixels in the given image. So, obviously, there is
a trade-off here. Dense techniques are more accurate, but they are slower. Sparse
techniques are less accurate, but they are faster. For real-time applications, people
tend to prefer sparse techniques. For applications where time and complexity is not a
factor, people prefer dense techniques to extract finer details.

In his paper, Farneback describes a method for dense optical flow estimation based on polynomial expansion for two frames. Our goal is to estimate the motion between these two frames, and it's basically a three-step process. In the first step, each neighborhood in both the frames is approximated by polynomials. In this case, we are only interested in quadratic polynomials. The next step is to construct a new signal by global displacement. Now that each neighborhood is approximated by a polynomial, we need to see what happens if this polynomial undergoes an ideal translation. The last step is to compute the global displacement by equating the coefficients in the yields of these quadratic polynomials.

Now, how is this feasible? If you think about it, we are assuming that an entire signal is a single polynomial and there is a global translation relating the two signals. This is not a realistic scenario. So, what are we looking for? Well, our goal is to find out whether these errors are small enough so that we can build a useful algorithm that can track the features.

Let's take a look at the following static image:

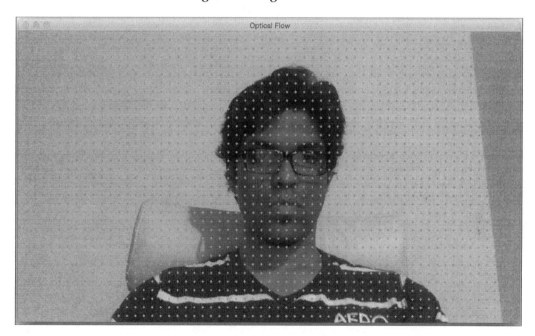

If I move sideways, you can see that the motion vectors point in the horizontal direction. They simply track the movement of my head:

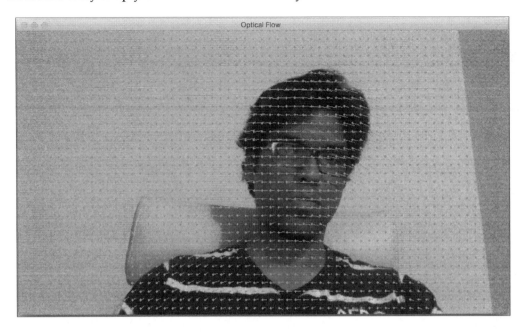

If I move away from the webcam, you can see that the motion vectors point in a direction that is perpendicular to the image plane:

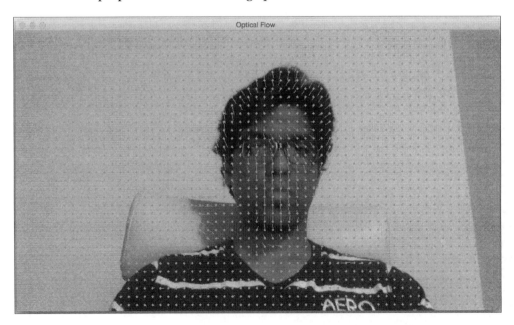

Here is the code used to perform optical flow-based tracking using the Farneback algorithm:

```cpp
int main(int, char** argv)
{
    // Variable declaration and initialization

    // Iterate until the user presses the Esc key
    while(true)
    {
        // Capture the current frame
        cap >> frame;

        if(frame.empty())
            break;

        // Resize the frame
        resize(frame, frame, Size(), scalingFactor, scalingFactor,
INTER_AREA);

        // Convert to grayscale
        cvtColor(frame, curGray, COLOR_BGR2GRAY);

        // Check if the image is valid
        if(prevGray.data)
        {
            // Initialize parameters for the optical flow algorithm
            float pyrScale = 0.5;
            int numLevels = 3;
            int windowSize = 15;
            int numIterations = 3;
            int neighborhoodSize = 5;
            float stdDeviation = 1.2;

            // Calculate optical flow map using Farneback algorithm
            calcOpticalFlowFarneback(prevGray, curGray, flowImage,
pyrScale, numLevels, windowSize, numIterations, neighborhoodSize,
stdDeviation, OPTFLOW_USE_INITIAL_FLOW);
```

As you can see, we use the Farneback algorithm to compute the optical flow vectors. The `calcOpticalFlowFarneback` input parameters are important when it comes to the quality of tracking. You can find the details about these parameters at http://docs.opencv.org/3.0-beta/modules/video/doc/motion_analysis_and_object_tracking.html. Let's go ahead and draw those vectors on the output image:

```cpp
        // Convert to 3-channel RGB
        cvtColor(prevGray, flowImageGray, COLOR_GRAY2BGR);

        // Draw the optical flow map
        drawOpticalFlow(flowImage, flowImageGray);

        // Display the output image
        imshow(windowName, flowImageGray);
    }

    // Break out of the loop if the user presses the Esc key
    ch = waitKey(10);
    if(ch == 27)
        break;

    // Swap previous image with the current image
    std::swap(prevGray, curGray);
    }

    return 1;
}
```

We used a function called `drawOpticalFlow` to draw these optical flow vectors. These vectors indicate the direction of the motion. Let's take a look at the function to see how we can draw these vectors:

```cpp
// Function to compute the optical flow map
void drawOpticalFlow(const Mat& flowImage, Mat& flowImageGray)
{
    int stepSize = 16;
    Scalar color = Scalar(0, 255, 0);

    // Draw the uniform grid of points on the input image along with
the motion vectors
    for(int y = 0; y < flowImageGray.rows; y += stepSize)
    {
        for(int x = 0; x < flowImageGray.cols; x += stepSize)
        {
```

```
            // Circles to indicate the uniform grid of points
            int radius = 2;
            int thickness = -1;
            circle(flowImageGray, Point(x,y), radius, color,
thickness);

            // Lines to indicate the motion vectors
            Point2f pt = flowImage.at<Point2f>(y, x);
            line(flowImageGray, Point(x,y), Point(cvRound(x+pt.x),
cvRound(y+pt.y)), color);
        }
    }
}
```

Summary

In this chapter, we learned about object tracking. We learned how to use the HSV colorspace to track colored objects. We discussed clustering techniques used for object tracking and how we can build an interactive object tracker using the CAMShift algorithm. We learned about corner detectors and how to track corners in a live video. We discussed how to track features in a video using optical flow. We also learned the concepts behind Lucas-Kanade and Farneback algorithms and implemented them as well.

In the next chapter, we will discuss segmentation algorithms and see how we can use them for text recognition.

10
Developing Segmentation Algorithms for Text Recognition

In the previous chapters, we learned about a wide range of image processing techniques, such as thresholding, contour descriptors, and mathematical morphology. In this chapter, we will discuss the common problems with dealing with scanned documents, such as identifying where the text is or adjusting its rotation. We will also learn how to combine techniques presented in the previous chapters to solve these problems. Finally, we'll have segmented regions of text that can be sent to an **OCR (optical character recognition)** library.

By the end of this chapter, you should be able to answer the following questions:

- What kind of OCR applications exist?
- What are the common problems while writing an OCR application?
- How do we identify regions of documents?
- How do we deal with problems such as skewing and other elements in the middle of the text?
- How do we use Tesseract OCR to identify the text?

Introducing optical character recognition

Identifying text in an image is a very popular application for Computer Vision. This process is commonly called OCR and divided into the following steps:

- **Text preprocessing and segmentation**: During this step, the computer must learn to deal with the image noise and rotation (skewing) and identify what areas are candidate text areas.

- **Text identification**: This is a process used to identify each letter in a text. Although this is also a Computer Vision topic, we will not show you how to do this in this book using OpenCV. Instead, we will show you how to use the Tesseract library to do this step, since it was integrated with OpenCV 3.0. If you are interested in learning how to do what Tesseract does all by yourself, take a look at *Mastering OpenCV, Packt Publishing*, which presents a chapter about car license plate recognition.

The preprocessing and segmentation phase can vary greatly depending on the source of the text. Let's take a look at the common situations where preprocessing is done:

- Production OCR applications with a scanner, which is a very reliable source of text: In this scenario, the background of the image is usually white and the document is almost aligned with the scanner margins. The content that is being scanned basically contains text with almost no noise. This kind of application relies on simple preprocessing techniques that can adjust the text quickly and maintain a fast scanning pace. When writing production OCR software, it is common to delegate identification of important text regions to the user and create a quality pipeline for text verification and indexing.

- Scanning text in a casually taken picture or in a video: This is a much more complex scenario, as there's no indication of where the text can be. This scenario is called *Scene text recognition*, and OpenCV 3.0 introduces a brand new library to deal with it, which we will cover in *Chapter 11, Text Recognition with Tesseract*. Usually, the preprocessor will use texture analysis techniques to identify the text patterns.

- Creating a production quality OCR for historical texts: Historical texts are also scanned.

  However, they have several additional problems, such as noise created by the old paper color and usage of ink. Other common problems are decorated letters, specific text fonts, and low-contrast content created by ink that has been degraded over time. It's not uncommon to write specific OCR software for documents at hand.

- Scanning maps, diagrams, and charts: Maps, diagrams, and charts pose a difficult scenario since the text is usually in any orientation and in the middle of an image's content. For example, city names are often clustered, and ocean names often follow country shore contour lines. Some charts are heavily colored, with text appearing in both clear and dark tones.

OCR application strategies also vary according to the objective of the identification. Will they be used for a full text search? Or should the text be separated in a logical field to index a database with information for a structured search?

In this chapter, we will focus on preprocessing scanned text or text photographed by a camera. We'll assume that the text is the main purpose of the image, such as in a photograph, paper, or card; for example, take a look at the following parking ticket:

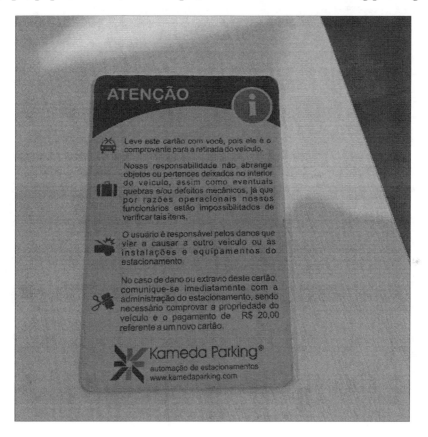

We'll try to remove the common noise, deal with text rotation (if any), and crop the possible text regions. While most OCR APIs already do these things automatically and probably with state-of-the-art algorithms, it still worth knowing how things happen under the hood. This will allow you to better understand most OCR APIs' parameters and will give you a better knowledge of potential OCR problems that you may face.

The preprocessing step

Software that identifies letters do so by comparing text with a previously recorded data. Classification results can be improved greatly if the input text is clear, if the letters are in a vertical position, and if there are no other elements, such as images that are sent to the classification software. In this section, we'll learn how to adjust text. This stage is called **preprocessing**.

Thresholding the image

We usually start the preprocessing stage by thresholding the image. This eliminates all the color information. Most OpenCV functions require information to be the written in white and the background to be black. So, let's start with creating a threshold function to match this criterion:

```cpp
#include <opencv2/opencv.hpp>
#include <vector>

using namespace std;
using namespace cv;

Mat binarize(Mat input)
{
  //Uses otsu to threshold the input image
  Mat binaryImage;
  cvtColor(input, input, CV_BGR2GRAY);
  threshold(input, binaryImage, 0, 255, THRESH_OTSU);
  //Count the number of black and white pixels
  int white = countNonZero(binaryImage);
  int black = binaryImage.size().area() - white;
  //If the image is mostly white (white background), invert it
  return white < black ? binaryImage : ~binaryImage;
}
```

The `binarize` function applies a threshold, similar to what we did in *Chapter 4,
Delving into Histograms and Filters*. However, we use the `Otsu` method by passing
`THRESH_OTSU` to the fourth parameter of the function.

The `Otsu` method maximizes the inter-class variance. Since a threshold creates only
two classes (the black and white pixels), this is the same as minimizing the intra-class
variance. The method works using the image histogram. Then, it iterates through all
the possible threshold values and calculates a measure of spread for the pixel values
on each side of the threshold, that is, the pixels that are either in the background or
in the foreground of the image. The purpose is to find the threshold value where the
sum of both the spreads is at its minimum.

After the thresholding is done, the function counts the number of white pixels in the
image. The black pixels are simply the total number of pixels in the image, given by
the image area minus the white pixel count.

Since text is usually written on a plain background, we will check whether there are
more white pixels than black. In this case, we are dealing with black text over a white
background, so we invert the image for further processing.

The result of the thresholding process with the parking ticket image is shown in the
following image:

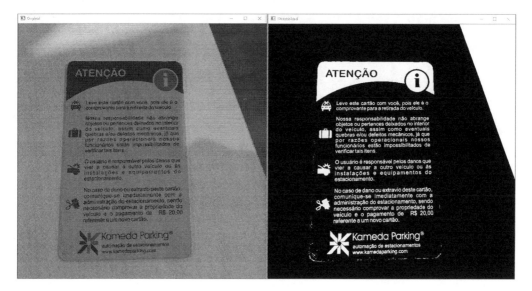

Text segmentation

The next step is to find where the text is located and extract it. There are two common strategies to do this, which are as follows:

- Using the connected component analysis, we search for groups of connected pixels in the image. This is the technique that we will use in this chapter.

- Use classifiers to search for a previously trained letter texture pattern. Texture features such as Haralick features and wavelet transforms are often used. The other option is to identify **maximally stable extremal regions (MSERs)** in this task. This approach is more robust for text in a complex background and will be studied in the next chapter. You can read about Haralick features on his own website at http://haralick.org/journals/ TexturalFeatures.pdf.

Creating connected areas

If you take a closer look at the image, you'll notice that the letters are always grouped together in blocks that are formed by each of text paragraphs. So, how do we detect and remove these blocks?

The first step is to make these blocks even more evident. We can do this using the dilation morphological operator. In *Chapter 8, Video Surveillance, Background Modeling, and Morphological Operations*, we learned how dilation makes the image elements thicker. Let's take a look at the following code snippet that does the trick:

```
Mat kernel = getStructuringElement(MORPH_CROSS, Size(3,3));
Mat dilated;
dilate(input, dilated, kernel, cv::Point(-1, -1), 5);
imshow("Dilated", dilated);
```

In this code, we start by creating a 3 x 3 cross kernel that will be used in the morphological operation. Then, we apply the dilation five times, centered on this kernel. The exact kernel size and number of times vary according to the situation. Just make sure that the values glue all the letters in the same line together.

The result of this operation is as follows:

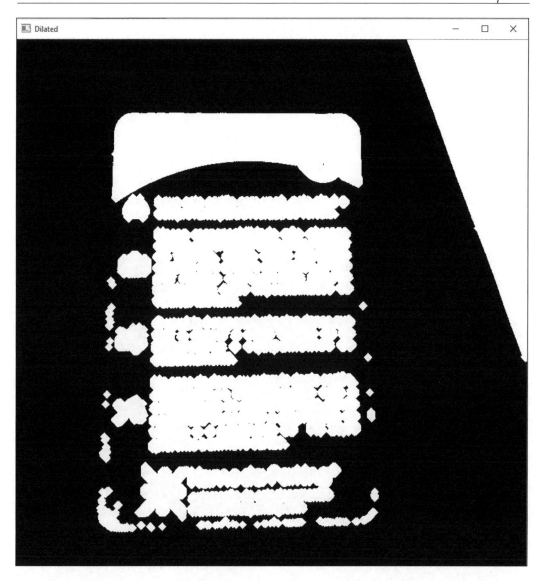

Notice that now we have huge white blocks. They exactly match each paragraph of the text and also match other nontextual elements such as images or the border noise.

The ticket image that comes with the code is a low resolution image. OCR engines usually work with high resolution images (200 or 300 DPI), so it may be necessary to apply dilation more than five times.

Identifying paragraph blocks

The next step is to perform connect component analysis to find blocks that correspond to paragraphs. OpenCV has a function to do this, which we previously used in *Chapter 5, Automated Optical Inspection, Object Segmentation, and Detection*. It's the findContours function:

```
vector<vector<Point> > contours;
findContours(dilated, contours, RETR_EXTERNAL, CHAIN_APPROX_SIMPLE);
```

In the first parameter, we pass our dilated image. The second parameter is the vector of detected contours. Then we use the option to retrieve only external contours and use simple approximation. The image contours are presented in the following figure. Each tone of gray represents a different contour:

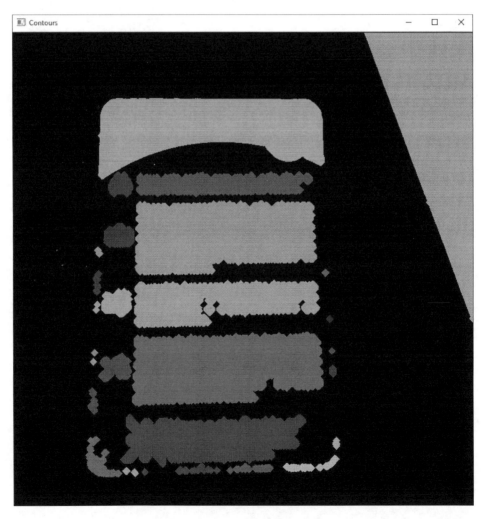

The last step is to identify the minimum rotated bounding rectangle of each contour. OpenCV provides a handy function for this operation called `minAreaRect`. This function receives a vector of arbitrary points and returns a `RoundedRect` that contains the bounding box.

This is also a good opportunity to discard unwanted rectangles, that is, rectangles that are obviously **not** text. Since we are making a software for OCR, we'll assume that the text contains a group of letters together. With this assumption, we'll discard text in the following situations:

- The rectangle width or size is too small, that is, smaller than 20 pixels. This will help you discard border noise and other small artifacts.

- The rectangles of the images that have a width/height proportion smaller than two. That is, rectangles that resemble a square, such as image icons, or ones that are much taller and larger will also be discarded.

There's a little caveat in the second condition. Since we are dealing with rotated bounding boxes, we must check whether the bounding box angle is not smaller than 45 degrees. If that's the case, the text will be vertically rotated, so the proportion that must be taken into account is the height/width. Let's take a look at this code:

```
//For each contour
vector<RotatedRect> areas;
for (auto contour : contours)
{
  //Find it's rotated rect
  auto box = minAreaRect(contour);

  //Discard very small boxes
  if (box.size.width < 20 || box.size.height < 20)
    continue;

  //Discard squares shaped boxes and boxes
  //higher than larger
  double proportion = box.angle < -45.0 ?
    box.size.height / box.size.width :
    box.size.width / box.size.height;
  if (proportion < 2)
    continue;
  //Add the box
  areas.push_back(box);
}
```

Let's see the boxes that are selected by this algorithm:

This is certainly a good result!

Notice that the algorithm described in condition 2 will also discard single letters. This is not a big issue, since we are creating an OCR preprocessor, and single symbols are usually meaningless with the context information. One example of such a case is the page numbers. They will be discarded with this process since they usually appear alone at the bottom of the page and will definitely fail the size or proportion text. However, this will not be a problem, as after the text passes through the OCR, there will be a huge text file with no page division at all.

We'll place this code in a function with this signature:

```
vector<RotatedRect> findTextAreas(Mat input)
```

Text extraction and skew adjustment

Now, all we need to do is extract the text and adjust text skew. This is done by the deskewAndCrop function, as follows:

```
Mat deskewAndCrop(Mat input, const RotatedRect& box)
{
  double angle = box.angle;
  Size2f size = box.size;

  //Adjust the box angle
   if (angle < -45.0)
  {
       angle += 90.0;
       std::swap(size.width, size.height);
  }

  //Rotate the text according to the angle
  Mat transform = getRotationMatrix2D(box.center, angle, 1.0);
  Mat rotated;
  warpAffine(input, rotated, transform, input.size(), INTER_CUBIC);

  //Crop the result
  Mat cropped;
  getRectSubPix(rotated, size, box.center, cropped);
  copyMakeBorder(cropped,cropped,10,10,10,10,BORDER_CONSTANT,
    Scalar(0));
  return cropped;
}
```

First, we start by reading the desired region, angle, and size. As mentioned earlier, the angle can be less than 45 degrees. This means that the text is vertically aligned, so we need to add 90 degrees to the rotation angle and switch the width and height properties.

Next, we need to rotate the text. First, we start by creating a 2D affine transformation matrix that describes the rotation. We do this using the `getRotationMatrix2D` OpenCV function. This function takes the following three parameters:

- CENTER: This is the central position of the rotation. The rotation will pivot around this center. In our case, we use the box center.

- ANGLE: This is the rotation angle. If the angle is negative, the rotation will occur in the clockwise direction.

- SCALE: This is an isotropic scale factor. We use 1.0 as we want to keep the box's original scale untouched.

The rotation itself is made using the `warpAffine` function. This function takes four mandatory arguments, which are as follows:

- SRC: This is the input `mat` array to be transformed.

- DST: This is the destination `mat` array.

- M: This is a transformation matrix. This matrix is a 2 x 3 affine transformation matrix. This may be a translation, scale, or rotation matrix. In our case, we just use the matrix that we recently created.

- SIZE: This is the size of the output image. We will generate an image with the same size as that of our input image.

The other three optional arguments are as follows:

- FLAGS: This indicates how the image should be interpolated. We use `BICUBIC_INTERPOLATION` for better quality. The default value is `LINEAR_INTERPOLATION`.

- BORDER: This is the border mode. We use the default `BORDER_CONSTANT`.

- BORDER VALUE: This is the color of the border. We use the default value, which is black.

Then, we use the `getRectSubPix` function. After we rotate our image, we need to crop the rectangular area of our bounding box. This function takes four mandatory arguments and one optional, and returns the cropped image:

- `IMAGE`: This is the image to be cropped.
- `SIZE`: This is a `cv::Size` object that describes the width and height of the box to be cropped.
- `CENTER`: This is the central pixel of the area to be cropped. Notice that as we rotate around the center, this point remains the same.
- `PATCH`: This is the destination image.
- `PATCH_TYPE`: This is the depth of the destination image. We use the default value, representing the same depth as that of the source image.

The final step is done by the `copyMakeBorder` function. This function adds a border around the image. This is important because the classification stage usually expects a margin around the text. The function parameters are very simple: the input and output images, the border thickness around the top, bottom, left, and right of the image, and the color of the new border.

For the card image, the following images will be generated:

Now, it's time to put every function together. Let's present the main method that will do the following:

- Load the ticket image
- Call our `binarization` function
- Find all text regions
- Show each region in a window:

```cpp
int main(int argc, char* argv[])
{
    //Loads the ticket image and binarize it
    Mat ticket = binarize(imread("ticket.png"));
    auto regions = findTextAreas(ticket);

    //For each region
    for (auto& region : regions) {
        //Crop
        auto cropped = deskewAndCrop(ticket, region);
        //Show
        imshow("Cropped text", cropped);
        waitKey(0);
        destroyWindow("Border Skew");
    }
}
```

 For the complete source code, take a look at the `segment.cpp` file that comes along with this book.

Installing Tesseract OCR on your operating system

Tesseract is an open source OCR engine originally developed by *Hewlett-Packard Laboratories, Bristol* and *Hewlett-Packard Co*. It has all the code licenses under the Apache License and is hosted on GitHub at `https://github.com/tesseract-ocr`.

It is considered one of the most accurate OCR engines that is available. It can read a wide variety of image formats and can convert text written in more than 60 languages.

In this session, we will teach you how to install Tesseract on Windows or Mac. Since there are lots of Linux distributions, we will not teach you how to install on this operating system.

Normally, Tesseract offers installation packages in your package repository, so before you compile Tesseract, just search there.

Installing Tesseract on Windows

Although Tesseract is hosted on GitHub, its latest Windows installer is still available in the old repository on Google Code. The latest installer version is 3.02.02, and it's recommended that you use the installer. Download the installer from `https://code.google.com/p/tesseract-ocr/downloads/list`.

Once you have downloaded the installer, perform these steps:

1. Look for the `tesseract-ocr-setup-3.02.02.exe` and `tesseract-3.02.02-win32-lib-include-dirs.zip` files, and download and run the executable installer

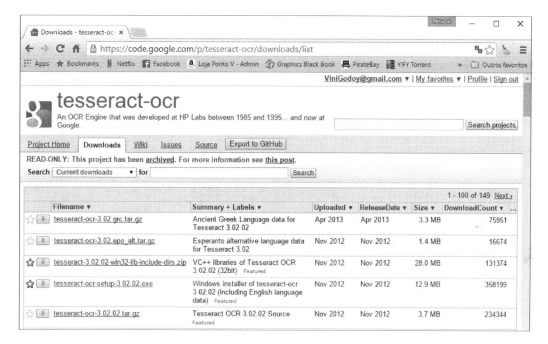

2. To get past the **welcome screen**, read and accept the license agreement.
3. Choose between installing for all users in the computer or just for your user.
4. Then, choose a suitable location for your installation.

5. Choose the folder of the installation. Tesseract points to the `program files` folder by default, since it has a command-line interface. You can change it to a more suitable folder, if you want. Then, go to the next screen:

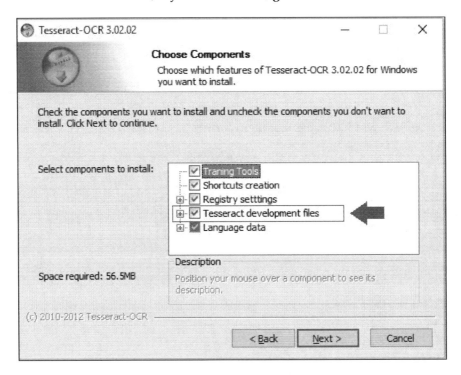

6. Make sure you select **Tesseract development files**. This will install the `Leptonica` library files and source code. You can also choose language data for your native language. Tesseract has English selected by default.

7. The installer will download and set up Tesseract dependencies.

To test the Tesseract installation, you can run it via the command line. For example, to run Tesseract on the `parkingTicket.png` file, you can run the following command:

```
tesseract parkingTicket.png ticket.txt
```

8. Now, go back to the downloaded `tesseract-3.02.02-win32-lib-include-dirs.zip` file. Unzip this file and copy the `lib` and `add` folders to your `tesseract` installation folder. There will be folders with the same name in this folder, but that's normal. This file will include `tesseract` files and libraries in the Tesseract installation. Ironically, Tesseract `libs` and `dlls` do not come with the installer.

Setting up Tesseract in Visual Studio

Since Visual Studio 2010 is the recommended IDE for Windows developers with Tesseract, it's important to set this up correctly.

The setup process is quite simple, and it's divided into the following three steps:

1. Adjust the import and library paths.
2. Add the libraries to the linker input.
3. Add Tesseract `dlls` to the windows path.

Let's see each of these steps in the following sections.

Setting the import and library paths

The import path tells Visual Studio where to search for the `.h` files that will be available when an `#include` directive is performed in your code.

In solution explorer, right-click on your **project** and click on **properties**. Then, select **configuration properties** and **VC++ Directories**.

 If you have created a new project from scratch, make sure you added at least one c++ file to the project to let Visual know that this is a C++ project.

Next, click on **Include Directories**. An arrow appears. Click on this arrow and then click on **Edit**:

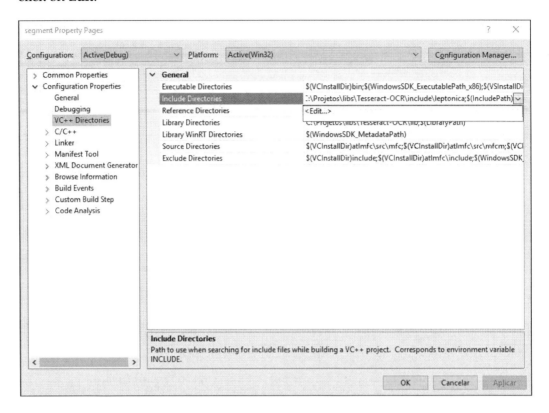

You must add two directories to this list:

```
TesseractInstallPath\include
TesseractInstallPath\include\leptonica
```

Replace the `TesseractInstallPath` with your Tesseract installation path; for example, `c:\Program Files\Tesseract-OCR`.

Then, click on **Library Directories**, click on the arrow, and then on `Edit`, just like you did for **Include Directories**. You must add one directory to the list:

```
TesseractInstallPath\lib
```

Configuring the linker

While still on the Property page, go to **Linker | Input**. Edit the **Additional Dependencies** row and include two libraries:

```
liblept168.lib
libtesseract302.lib
```

Since the numbers in the `lib` name refer to the file version, the library names can change if you install a different version of Tesseract. To do this, just open the `lib` path in Windows Explorer.

Unfortunately, the debug libraries (the ones that end with a *d* letter) do not work out of the box with Tesseract. If you really need to use them, you need to compile Tesseract and Leptonica yourself.

Adding the libraries to the windows path

You must add two library files to the windows path. The first is located directly in `TesseractInstallPath` and it is called `liblept168.dll`. The second one is in `TesseractInstallPath\lib` and it is called `libtesseract302.dll`. There are two ways to do this:

- Copy these files to a location where Visual Studio generates your executable file. This will not add the files to the Windows path but will allow the application to run.

- Copy these files to a folder that is configured in the Windows path. You can configure a new folder in the Windows path by changing the environment variables in **System Properties**.

Some internet tutorials teach you to include these files in folders, such as `Windows\System32`. Do not do this. If you do this, it can be hard to change the library version in the future, since this folder has a lot of other `dlls` systems, and you may lose track of what you already placed in there. Also, you can always disable a custom path to test an installer and check whether you forgot to pack a `dll` in your installation bundle.

Installing Tesseract on Mac

The easiest way to install Tesseract OCR on Mac is using Homebrew. If you don't have Homebrew installed, just go to the Homebrew site (http://brew.sh/), open your console, and run the Ruby script that is on the front page. You may be required to type your administrator password.

After homebrew is installed, just type the following command:

```
brew install tesseract
```

The English language is already included in this installation. If you want to install other language packs, just run the following command:

```
brew install tesseract --all-languages
```

This will install all language packs. Then, just go to the Tesseract installation directory and delete all unwanted languages. Homebrew usually installs stuff in /usr/local/.

Using Tesseract OCR library

As Tesseract OCR is already integrated with OpenCV 3.0, it still worth studying its API since it allows a finer-grained control over Tesseract parameters. The integration will be studied in the next chapter.

Creating a OCR function

We'll change the previous example to work with Tesseract. We will start with adding baseapi and fstream tesseracts to the list:

```
#include <opencv2/opencv.hpp>
#include <tesseract/baseapi.h>

#include <vector>
#include <fstream>
```

Then, we'll create a global TessBaseAPI object that represents our Tesseract OCR engine:

```
tesseract::TessBaseAPI ocr;
```

The ocr engine is completely self-contained. If you want to create multithreaded OCR software, just add a different `TessBaseAPI` object to each thread, and the execution will be fairly thread-safe. You just need to guarantee that file writing is not done over the same file; otherwise, you'll need to guarantee safety for this operation.

Next, we will create a function called `identify` text that will run the OCR:

```
char* identifyText(Mat input, char* language = "eng")
{
  ocr.Init(NULL, language, tesseract::OEM_TESSERACT_ONLY);
  ocr.SetPageSegMode(tesseract::PSM_SINGLE_BLOCK);
  ocr.SetImage(input.data, input.cols, input.rows, 1,
    input.step);
  char* text = ocr.GetUTF8Text();
  cout << "Text:" << endl;
  cout << text << endl;
  cout << "Confidence: " << ocr.MeanTextConf() << endl << endl;

    // Get the text
  return text;
}
```

Let's explain this function line by line. In the first line, we start initializing Tesseract. This is done by calling the `init` function. This function has the following signature:

```
int Init(const char* datapath, const char* language,
    OcrEngineMode oem)
```

Let's explain each parameter:

- **Datapath**: This is the path to the `tessdata` files of the root directory. The path must end with a backslash / character. The `tessdata` directory contains the language files that you installed. Passing NULL to this parameter will make Tesseract search in its installation directory, which is the location where this folder is normally present. It's common to change this value to `args[0]` when deploying an application and include the `tessdata` folder in your application path.

- **Language**: This is a three-letter word with the language code (for example, eng for English, por for Portuguese, or hin for Hindi). Tesseract supports loading of multiple language code using the + sign. So, passing *eng + por* will load both English and Portuguese. Of course, you can only use languages that you have previously installed; otherwise, the loading will fail. A language config file can specify that two or more languages must be loaded together. To prevent this, you can use a tilde ~. For example, you can use hin+~eng to guarantee that English is not loaded with Hindi, even if it is configured to do so.

- **OcrEngineMode**: These are OCR algorithms that will be used. They can have one of the following values:

  ○ OEM_TESSERACT_ONLY: This uses just Tesseract. It's the fastest method, but it also has less precision.

  ○ OEM_CUBE_ONLY: This uses cube engine. It's slower, but it's more precise. This will only work if your language was trained to support this engine mode. To check whether that's the case, look for .cube files for your language in the tessdata folder. The support for English is guaranteed.

  ○ OEM_TESSERACT_CUBE_COMBINED: This combines both Tesseract and Cube in order to achieve the best possible OCR classification. This engine has the best accuracy and the slowest execution time.

  ○ OEM_DEFAULT: This tries to infer the strategy based on the language config file and the command line config file, or in the absence of both, uses OEM_TESSERACT_ONLY.

It's important to emphasize that the init function *can* be executed many times. If a different language or engine mode is provided, Tesseract will clear the previous configuration and start again. If the same parameters are provided, Tesseract is smart enough to simply ignore the command. The init function returns 0 for success and -1 for failure.

Our program then proceeds by setting the page segmentation mode:

```
ocr.SetPageSegMode(tesseract::PSM_SINGLE_BLOCK);
```

There are several segmentation modes available, which are as follows:

- PSM_OSD_ONLY: Using this mode, Tesseract just runs its preprocessing algorithms to detect the orientation and script detection.

- PSM_AUTO_OSD: This tells Tesseract to perform automatic page segmentation with orientation and script detection.

- PSM_AUTO_ONLY: This does page segmentation, but avoids doing orientation, script detection, or OCR.

- PSM_AUTO: This does page segmentation and OCR, but avoids doing orientation or script detection.

- PSM_SINGLE_COLUMN: This assumes that the text of variable sizes is displayed in a single column.

- PSM_SINGLE_BLOCK_VERT_TEXT: This treats the image as a single uniform block of a vertically aligned text.

- PSM_SINGLE_BLOCK: This is a single block of text. This is the default configuration. We will use this flag since our preprocessing phase guarantees this condition.

- PSM_SINGLE_LINE: This indicates that the image contains only one line of text.

- PSM_SINGLE_WORD: This indicates that the image contains just one word.

- PSM_SINGLE_WORD_CIRCLE: This indicates that the image is just one word that is disposed in a circle.

- PSM_SINGLE_CHAR: This indicates that the image contains a single character.

Notice that Tesseract has already implemented deskewing and text segmentation algorithms, as most OCR libraries do. But it's interesting to know such algorithms as you can provide your own preprocessing phase for specific needs. This allows you to improve text detection is many cases. For example, if you are creating an OCR application for old documents, the default threshold used by Tesseract can create a dark background. Tesseract may also be confused by borders or severe text skewing.

Next, we call the SetImage method with the signature:

```
void SetImage(const unsigned char* imagedata, int width,
    int height, int bytes_per_pixel, int bytes_per_line);
```

The parameters are almost self-explanatory, and most of them can be read directly from our mat object:

- data: This is a raw byte array that contains the image data. OpenCV contains a function called data() in the Mat class that provides a direct pointer to the data.

- width: This is the image width.

- height: This is the image height.

- `bytes_per_pixel`: This is the number of bytes per pixel. We use 1, since we are dealing with a binary image. If you want to allow the code to be more generic, you can also use the `Mat::elemSize()` function that provides the same information.

- `bytes_per_line`: This is the number of bytes in a single line. We use the `Mat::step` property since some images add trailing bytes.

Then, we call `GetUTF8Text` to run the recognition itself. The recognized text is returned, encoded with UTF8 without BOM (byte order mark). Before we return it, we also print some debug information.

The `MeanTextConf` returns a confidence index, which can be a number from 0 to 100:

```
char* text = ocr.GetUTF8Text();
cout << "Text:" << endl;
cout << text << endl;
cout << "Confidence: " << ocr.MeanTextConf() << endl << endl;
```

Sending the output to a file

Let's change our `main` method to send the recognized output to a file. We do this using a standard `ofstream`:

```
int main(int argc, char* argv[])
{
  //Loads the ticket image and binarize it
  Mat ticket = binarize(imread("ticket.png"));
  auto regions = findTextAreas(ticket);

  std::ofstream file;
  file.open("ticket.txt", std::ios::out | std::ios::binary);

  //For each region
  for (auto region : regions) {
    //Crop
    auto cropped = deskewAndCrop(ticket, region);
    char* text = identifyText(cropped, "por");

    file.write(text, strlen(text));
    file << endl;
  }

  file.close();
}
```

Notice the following line:

```
file.open("ticket.txt", std::ios::out | std::ios::binary);
```

This opens the file in binary mode. This is important since Tesseract returns a text encoded in UTF-8, taking into account the special characters available in Unicode. We also write the output directly using the following command:

```
file.write(text, strlen(text));
```

In this sample, we called `identify` using Portuguese as the input language (this is the language in which the ticket was written). You can use another photo, if you like.

 The complete source file is provided in the `segmentOcr.cpp` file, which comes along with this book.

 `ticket.png` is a low resolution image, since we imagined that you would want to display a window with the image while studying this code. For this image, Tesseract results are rather poor. If you want to test it with a higher resolution image, the code is provided with a `ticketHigh.png` image. To test this image, change the dilation repetitions to 12 and the minimum box size from 20 to 60. You'll get a much higher confidence rate (about 87%) and the resulting text will be fully readable. The `segmentOcrHigh.cpp` file contains these modifications.

Summary

In this chapter, we presented a brief introduction to OCR applications. We saw that the preprocessing phase of such systems must be adjusted according to the type of documents that we are planning to identify. We learned the common operations while preprocessing text files, such as thresholding, cropping, skewing, and text region segmentation. Finally, we learned how to install and use Tesseract OCR to convert our image to text.

In the next chapter, we'll use a more sophisticated OCR technique to identify text in a casually taken picture or video—a situation known as scene text recognition. This is a much more complex scenario, since the text can be anywhere, in any font, and with different illuminations and orientations. There can be no text at all! We'll also learn how to use the OpenCV 3.0 text contribution module, which is fully integrated with Tesseract.

11
Text Recognition with Tesseract

In the previous chapter, we covered the very basic OCR processing functions. Although they are quite useful for scanned or photographed documents, they are almost useless when dealing with text that casually appears in a picture.

In this chapter, we'll explore the OpenCV 3.0 text module, which deals specifically with scene text detection. Using this API, it is possible to detect text that appears in a webcam video, or to analyze photographed images (like the ones in Street View or taken by a surveillance camera) to extract text information in real time. This allows a wide range of applications to be created, from accessibility to marketing and even robotics fields.

By the end of this chapter, you will be able to:

- Understand what is scene text recognition
- Understand how the text API works
- Use the OpenCV 3.0 text API to detect text
- Extract the detected text to an image
- Use the text API and Tesseract integration to identify letters

How the text API works

The text API implements the algorithm proposed by Lukás Neumann and Jiri Matas in the article called *Real-Time Scene Text Localization and Recognition* during the **CVPR (Computer Vision and Pattern Recognition)** Conference in 2012. This algorithm represented a significant increase in scene text detection, performing the state-of-the art detection both in the CVPR database as well as in the Google Street View database.

Before we use the API, let's take a look at how this algorithm works under the hood, and how it addresses the scene text detection problem.

> **Remember** that the OpenCV 3.0 text API does not come with the standard OpenCV modules. It's an additional module present in the OpenCV contribute package. If you need to install OpenCV using the Windows Installer, refer to *Chapter 1, Getting Started with OpenCV*, which will help you install these modules.

The scene detection problem

Detecting text that randomly appears in a scene is a problem harder than it looks. There are several new variables when we compare them to identify scanned text, which are as follows:

- **Tri-dimensionality**: The text can be in any scale, orientation, or perspective. Also, the text can be partially occluded or interrupted. There are literally thousands of possible regions where it can appear in the image.

- **Variety**: Text can be in several different fonts and colors. The font can have outline borders or not. The background can be a dark, light, or a complex image.

- **Illumination and shadows**: The sunlight position and apparent color changes over the time. Different weather conditions such as fog or rain can generate noise. Illumination can be a problem even in closed spaces, since light reflects over colored objects and hits the text.

- **Blurring**: Text can appear in a region that is not prioritized by the auto focus lenses. Blurring is also common in moving cameras, in perspective text, or in the presence of fog.

The following image, taken from Google Street View, illustrates these problems. Notice how several of these situations occur simultaneously in just a single image:

Performing a text detection to deal with such situations may prove computationally expensive, since there are *2n* subsets of pixels where the text can be, *n* being the number of pixels in the image.

In order to reduce the complexity, two strategies are commonly applied, which are as follows:

- Use a sliding window to search a subset of image rectangles. This strategy just reduces the number of subsets to a smaller amount. The amount of regions varies according to the complexity of text being considered. Algorithms that deal just with text rotation can use small values, as compared to the ones that also deal with rotation, skewing, perspective, and so on. The advantage of this approach is its simplicity, but it is usually limited to a narrow range of fonts, and often, to a lexicon of specific words.

- Use of the connected component analysis. This approach assumes that pixels can be grouped into regions where pixels have similar properties. These regions are supposed to have higher chances of being identified as characters. The advantage of this approach is that it does not depend on several text properties (orientation, scale, and fonts), and they also provide a segmentation region that can be used to crop text to the OCR. This was the approach used in the previous chapter.

- The OpenCV 3.0 algorithm uses the second one by performing the connected component analysis and searching for extremal regions.

Extremal regions

Extremal regions are connected areas that are characterized by uniform intensity and surrounded by a contrast background. The stability of a region can be measured by calculating how resistant the region is to the thresholding variance. This variance can be measured with a simple algorithm:

1. Applying the threshold generates an image A. Detect its connected pixel regions (extremal regions).

2. Increasing the threshold by a delta amount generates an image B. Detect its connected pixel regions (extremal regions).

3. Compare image B with A. If a region in image A is similar to the same region in image B, then add it to the same branch in the tree. The criteria of similarity may vary from implementation to implementation, but it's usually related to the image area or general shape. If a region in image A appears to be split in image B, create two new branches in the tree for the new regions, and associate them with the previous branch.

4. Set *A* = *B* and go back to step 2, until a maximum threshold is applied.

This will assemble a tree of regions, as shown in the following figure:

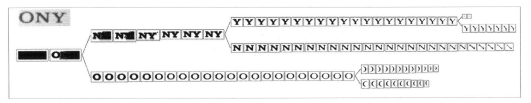

Image source: `http://docs.opencv.org/master/da/d56/group__text__detect.html#gsc.tab=0`

The resistance to variance is determined by counting the number of nodes that are in the same level.

By analyzing this tree, it's also possible to determine the **MSERs (Maximally Stable Extremal Regions)**, that is, the regions where the area remains stable in a wide variety of thresholds. In the previous image, it is clear that these areas will contain the letters *O*, *N*, and *Y*. The main disadvantage of MSERs is that they are weak in the presence of blur. OpenCV provides a MSER feature detector in the `feature2d` module.

Extremal regions are interesting because they are strongly invariant to illumination, scale, and orientation. They are also good candidates for text because they are also invariant of the type of font used, even when the font is styled. Each region can also be analyzed in order to determine its boundary ellipsis and have properties, such as affine transformation and area that can be numerically determined. Finally, it's worth mentioning that this entire process is fast, which makes it a very good candidate for real-time applications.

Extremal region filtering

Although MSERs are a common approach to define which extremal regions are worth working with, the Neumann and Matas algorithm uses a different approach by submitting all extremal regions to a sequential classifier that is trained for character detection. This classifier works in the following two different stages:

- The first stage incrementally computes descriptors (the bounding box, perimeter, area, and Euler number) for each region. These descriptors are submitted to a classifier that estimates how probable the region is for it to be a character in the alphabet. Then, only the regions of high probability are selected to stage 2.

- In this stage, the features of the whole area ratio, convex hull ratio, and the number of outer boundary inflexion points are calculated. This provides a more detailed information that allows the classifier to discard `nontext` characters, but they are also much slower to calculate.

In OpenCV, this process is implemented in an `ERFilter` class. It is also possible to use different image single-channel projections such as R, G, B, luminance, or grayscale conversion to increase the character recognition rates.

Finally, all the characters must be grouped in text blocks (such as words or paragraphs). OpenCV 3.0 provides two algorithms for this purpose:

- **Prune Exhaustive Search**: This was also proposed by Mattas in 2011. This algorithm does not need any previous training or classification, but is limited to a horizontally aligned text.

- **Hierarchical Method for Oriented Text**: This deals with texts in any orientation, but needs a trained classifier.

Since these operations require classifiers, it is also necessary to provide a trained set as an input. OpenCV3.0 provides some of these trained sets in the `sample` package. This also means that this algorithm is sensitive to the fonts used in classifier training.

A demonstration of this algorithm can be seen in the video provided by Neumann at `https://youtu.be/ejd5gGea2Fo`.

Once the text is segmented, it just needs to be sent to an OCR, such as Tesseract, similar to what we did in the previous chapter. The only difference is that now we will use OpenCV text module classes to interact with Tesseract, since they provide a way to encapsulate the specific OCR engine we are using.

Using the text API

Enough of theory. It's time to see how the text module works in practice. Let's study how to use it to perform text detection, extraction, and identification.

Text detection

Let's start with creating a simple program to perform text segmentation using `ERFilters`. In this program, we will use the trained classifiers from text API samples. You can download them from the OpenCV repository, but they are also available in the book's companion code.

First, we start with including all the necessary `libs` and using:

```
#include    "opencv2/highgui.hpp"
#include    "opencv2/imgproc.hpp"
#include    "opencv2/text.hpp"

#include    <vector>
#include    <iostream>

using namespace std;
using namespace cv;
using namespace cv::text;
```

Recall from our previous section that the `ERFilter` works separately in each image channel. So, we must provide a way to separate each desired channel in a different single `cv::Mat` channel. This is done by the `separateChannels` function:

```cpp
vector<Mat> separateChannels(Mat& src)
{
  vector<Mat> channels;
  //Grayscale images
  if (src.type() == CV_8U || src.type() == CV_8UC1) {
    channels.push_back(src);
    channels.push_back(255-src);
    return channels;
  }

  //Colored images
  if (src.type() == CV_8UC3) {
    computeNMChannels(src, channels);
    int size = static_cast<int>(channels.size())-1;
    for (int c = 0; c < size; c++)
      channels.push_back(255-channels[c]);
    return channels;
  }

  //Other types
  cout << "Invalid image format!" << endl;
  exit(-1);
}
```

First, we verify that the image is a single channel image (for example, a grayscale image). If that's the case, we just add this image and its negative to be processed.

Otherwise, we check whether it's an RGB image. For colored images, we call the computeNMChannels to split the image in its several channels. The function is defined as follows:

```
void computeNMChannels(InputArray src, OutputArrayOfArrays channels,
int mode = ERFILTER_NM_RGBLGrad);
```

Its parameters are described as follows:

- src: This is the source input array. It should be a colored image of type 8UC3.

- channels: This is a vector of mats that will be filled with the resulting channels.

- mode: This defines the channels that will be computed. There are two possible values that can be used, which are as follows:

- ERFILTER_NM_RGBLGrad: This indicates that the algorithm uses an RGB color, lightness, and gradient magnitude as channels (default).

- ERFILTER_NM_IHSGrad: This indicates that the image will be split by its intensity, hue, saturation, and gradient magnitude.

We also append the negatives of all color components in the vector. Finally, if another kind of image is provided, the function will terminate the program with an error message.

 Negatives are appended so the algorithms will cover both bright text on a dark background and dark text on a bright background. There is no point in adding a negative to the gradient magnitude.

Let's proceed to the `main` method. We'll use the program to segment the `easel.png` image, which is provided with the source code:

This image was taken by a mobile phone camera, while I was walking on the street. Let's code so that you can also use a different image easily by providing its name in the first program argument:

```
int main(int argc, const char * argv[])
{
  char* image = argc < 2 ? "easel.png" : argv[1];
   auto input = imread(image);
```

Next, we'll convert the image to grayscale and separate its channels by calling the `separateChannels` function:

```
 Mat processed;
  cvtColor(input, processed, CV_RGB2GRAY);
 auto channels = separateChannels(processed);
```

If you want to work with all the channels in a colored image, just replace the first two lines of the preceding code with the following code:

```
Mat processed = input;
```

We will need to analyze six channels (RGB + inverted) instead of two (gray + inverted). Actually the processing time will increase much more than the improvements that we can get.With the channels in hand, we need to create ERFilters for both the stages of the algorithm. Luckily, the opencv text contribution module provides functions for this:

```
// Create ERFilter objects with the 1st and 2nd stage classifiers
auto filter1 = createERFilterNM1(
    loadClassifierNM1("trained_classifierNM1.xml"),  15, 0.00015f,
      0.13f, 0.2f,true,0.1f);

auto filter2 = createERFilterNM2(
   loadClassifierNM2("trained_classifierNM2.xml"),0.5);
```

For the first stage, we call the loadClassifierNM1 function to load a previously trained classification model. The XML containing the training data is its only argument. Then, we call createERFilterNM1 to create an instance of the ERFilter class that will perform the classification. The function has the following signature:

```
Ptr<ERFilter> createERFilterNM1(const Ptr<ERFilter::Callback>& cb,
    int thresholdDelta = 1,
    float minArea = 0.00025, float maxArea = 0.13,
    float minProbability = 0.4, bool nonMaxSuppression = true,
    float minProbabilityDiff = 0.1);
```

The parameters are described as follows:

- cb: This is the classification model. This is the same model that we loaded with the loadCassifierNM1 function.

- thresholdDelta: This is the amount to be added to the threshold in each algorithm iteration. The default value is *1*, but we'll use *15* in our example.

- minArea: This is the minimum area of the ER where text can be found. This is measured in % of the image size. ERs with areas smaller than this are immediately discarded.

- maxArea: This is the maximum area of the ER where text can be found. This is also measured in % of the image size. ERs with areas greater than this are immediately discarded.

- minProbability: This is the minimum probability that a region must have to be a character in order to remain for the next stage.

- `nonMaxSupression`: This indicates that non-maximum suppression will be done in each branch probability.
- `minProbabilityDiff`: This is the minimum probability difference between the minimum and maximum extreme region.

The process for the second stage is similar. We call `loadClassifierNM2` to load the classifier model for the second stage and `createERFilterNM2` to create the second stage classifier. This function only takes the loaded classification model and a minimum probability that a region must achieve to be considered a character as input parameters.

So, let's call these algorithms in each channel to identify all possible text regions:

```
//Extract text regions using Newmann & Matas algorithm
cout << "Processing " << channels.size() << " channels...";
cout << endl;
vector<vector<ERStat> > regions(channels.size());
for (int c=0; c < channels.size(); c++)
{
    cout << "    Channel " << (c+1) << endl;
    filter1->run(channels[c], regions[c]);
    filter2->run(channels[c], regions[c]);
}
filter1.release();
filter2.release();
```

In the previous code, we used the `run` function of the `ERFilter` class. This function takes the following two arguments:

- **The input channel**: This is the image to be processed.
- **The regions**: In the first stage algorithm, this argument will be filled with the detected regions. In the second stage (performed by `filter2`), this argument must contain the regions selected in stage 1, which will be processed and filtered by stage 2.

Finally, we release both the filters, since they will not be needed anymore in the program.

The final segmentation step is to group all `ERRegions` into possible words and define their bounding boxes. This is done by calling the `erGrouping` function:

```
//Separate character groups from regions
vector< vector<Vec2i> > groups;
vector<Rect> groupRects;
erGrouping(input, channels, regions, groups, groupRects, ERGROUPING_
ORIENTATION_HORIZ);
```

This function has the following signature:

```
void erGrouping(InputArray img, InputArrayOfArrays channels,
    std::vector<std::vector<ERStat> > &regions,
    std::vector<std::vector<Vec2i> > &groups,
    std::vector<Rect> &groups_rects,
    int method = ERGROUPING_ORIENTATION_HORIZ,
    const std::string& filename = std::string(),
    float minProbablity = 0.5);
```

Let's take a look at the definition of each parameter:

- `img`: This is the original input image. You can refer to the following observations.

- `regions`: This is a vector of single-channel images where regions are extracted.

- `groups`: This is an output vector of indexes of grouped regions. Each group region contains all extremal regions of a single word.

- `groupRects`: This is a list of rectangles with the detected text regions.

- `method`: This is a method of grouping. It can be as follows:

    - `ERGROUPING_ORIENTATION_HORIZ`: This is the default value. This only generates groups with horizontally oriented text by performing an exhaustive search, as proposed originally by Neumann and Matas.

    - `ERGROUPING_ORIENTATION_ANY`: This generates groups with text in any orientation, using **Single Linkage Clustering** and **classifiers**. If you use this method, the filename of the classifier model must be provided in the next parameter.

    - `Filename`: This is the name of the classifier model. It is only needed if `ERGROUPING_ORIENTATION_ANY` is selected.

    - `minProbability`: This is the minimum detected probability of accepting a group. Also, it is only needed if the `ERGROUPING_ORIENTATION_ANY` is used.

The code also provides a call to the second method, but it's commented. You can switch between the two to test it. Just comment the previous call and uncomment this one:

```
erGrouping(input, channels, regions,
    groups, groupRects, ERGROUPING_ORIENTATION_ANY,
    "trained_classifier_erGrouping.xml", 0.5);
```

For this call, we also used the default trained classifier provided in the text module sample package.

Finally, we draw the region boxes and show the results:

```
// draw groups boxes
for (auto rect : groupRects)
    rectangle(input, rect, Scalar(0, 255, 0), 3);
imshow("grouping",input);
waitKey(0);
```

The output of the program is shown in the following image:

You can check the complete source code in the detection.cpp file.

> While most OpenCV text module functions are written to support both grayscale and colored images as their input parameters, by the time this book was written, there were bugs that prevented using grayscale images in functions, such as erGrouping; for instance. Refer to https://github.com/Itseez/opencv_contrib/issues/309.
>
> Always remember that the OpenCV contribute modules package is not as stable as the default opencv packages.

Text extraction

Now that we detected the regions, we must crop the text before we submit it to the OCR. We can simply use a function such as getRectSubpix or Mat::copy using each region rectangle as a **ROI (region of interest)**, but since the letters are skewed, some undesired text may be cropped as well; for instance, this is what one of the regions will look like if we just extract the ROI based in its given rectangle:

Fortunately, the ERFilter provides us with an object called ERStat, which contains pixels inside each extremal region. With these pixels, we can use the OpenCV floodFill function to reconstruct each letter. This function is capable of painting similar colored pixels based in a seed point, just like the bucket tool of most drawing applications. This is what the function signature looks like:

```
int floodFill(InputOutputArray image, InputOutputArray mask,
    Point seedPoint, Scalar newVal,
    CV_OUT Rect* rect=0,
    Scalar loDiff = Scalar(), Scalar upDiff = Scalar(),
    int flags = 4
);
```

Let's understand these parameters and see how they can be used:

*   image: This is the input image. We'll use the channel image where the extremal region was taken. This is where the function normally does the flood fill, unless the FLOODFILL_MASK_ONLY is supplied. In this case, the image remains untouched and the drawing occurs in the mask. That's exactly what we will do.

- `mask`: The mask must be an image two rows and columns greater than the input image. When flood fill draws a pixel, it verifies that the corresponding pixel in the mask is zero. In that case, it will draw and mark this pixel as one (or the other value passed in the flags). If the pixel is not zero, flood fill does not paint the pixel. In our case, we'll provide a blank mask, so every letter will get painted in the mask.

- `seedPoint`: This is the starting point. It's similar to the place where you click when you want to use the "bucket" tool of a graphic application.

- `newVal`: This is the new value of the repainted pixels.

- `loDiff` and `upDiff`: These parameters represent the lower and upper difference between the pixels being processed and their neighbors. The neighbor will be painted if it falls in this range. If the FLOODFILL_FIXED_ RANGE flag is used, the difference between the seed point and the pixels being processed will be used instead.

- `rect`: This is the optional parameter that limits the region where the flood fill will be applied.

- `flags`: This value is represented by a bit mask.

    - The least significant eight bits of the flag contain a connectivity value. A value of 4 indicates that all the four edge pixels will be used, and a value of 8 will indicates that diagonal pixels must also be taken into account. We'll use four for this parameter.

    - The next 8 to 16 bits contain a value from 1 to 255 and are used to fill the mask. Since we want to fill the mask with white, we'll use 255 << 8 for this value.

    - There are two more bits that can be set by adding the FLOODFILL_ FIXED_RANGE and FLOODFILL_MASK_ONLY flags, as described earlier.

We'll create a function called drawER. This function will receive four parameters:

- A vector with all processed channels
- The ERStat regions
- The group that must be drawn
- The group rectangle

This function will return an image with the word represented by this group. Let's start with this function by creating the mask image and defining the flags:

```
Mat out = Mat::zeros(channels[0].rows+2, channels[0].cols+2, CV_8UC1);
int flags = 4                        //4 neighbors
  + (255 << 8)                       //paint mask in white (255)
  + FLOODFILL_FIXED_RANGE            //fixed range
  + FLOODFILL_MASK_ONLY;             //Paint just the mask
```

Then, we'll loop though each group. It's necessary to find the region index and its stats. There's a chance that this extreme region will be the root, which does not contain any points. In this case, we'll just ignore it:

```
for (int g=0; g < group.size(); g++)
{
int idx = group[g][0];
    ERStat er = regions[idx][group[g][1]];
//Ignore root region
    if (er.parent == NULL)
      continue;
```

Now, we can read the pixel coordinate from the ERStat object. It's represented by the pixel number, counting from top to bottom, left to right. This linear index must be converted to a *row (y)* and *column (z)* notation, using a formula similar to the one that we discussed in *Chapter 2, An Introduction to the Basics of OpenCV*:

```
int px = er.pixel % channels[idx].cols;
int py = er.pixel / channels[idx].cols;
Point p(px, py);
```

Then, we can call the floodFill function. The ERStat object gives us the value that we need to use in the loDiff parameter:

```
floodFill(
    channels[idx], out,          //Image and mask
    p, Scalar(255),              //Seed and color
    nullptr,                      /No rect
    Scalar(er.level),Scalar(0),   //LoDiff and upDiff
    flags                         //Flags
```

After we do this for all regions in the group, we'll end it with an image a little bigger than the original one, with a black background and the word in white letters. Now, let's crop just the area of the letters. Since the region rectangle was given, we start with defining it as our region of interest:

```
out = out(rect);
```

Then, we'll find all nonzero pixels. This is the value that we'll use in the `minAreaRect` function to get the rotated rectangle around the letters. Finally, we borrow the previous chapter's `deskewAndCrop` function to crop and rotate the image for us:

```
vector<Point> points;
findNonZero(out, points);
//Use deskew and crop to crop it perfectly
return deskewAndCrop(out, minAreaRect(points));
}
```

This is the result of the process for the easel image:

Text recognition

In *Chapter 10, Developing Segmentation Algorithms for Text Recognition*, we used the Tesseract API directly to recognize the text regions. This time, we'll use OpenCV classes to accomplish the same goal.

In OpenCV, all OCR-specific classes are derived from the `BaseOCR` virtual class. This class provides a common interface for the OCR execution method itself.

Specific implementations must inherit from this class. By default, the text module provides three different implementations: `OCRTesseract`, `OCRHMMDecoder`, and `OCRBeamSearchDecoder`.

This hierarchy is depicted in the following class diagram:

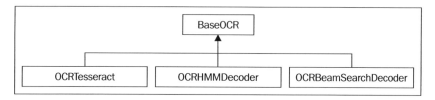

With this approach, we can separate the part of the code where the OCR mechanism is created from the execution itself. This makes it easier to change the OCR implementation in the future.

So, let's start with creating a method that decides which implementation we'll use based on a string. We will currently support Tesseract. However, you can take a look at the chapter code where a demonstration with `HMMDecoder` is also provided. We are also accepting the OCR engine name in a string parameter, but we can improve our application flexibility by reading it from an external JSON or XML configuration file:

```
cv::Ptr<BaseOCR> initOCR2(const string& ocr)
{
  if (ocr == "tesseract") {
    return OCRTesseract::create(nullptr, "eng+por");
  }
  throw string("Invalid OCR engine: ") + ocr;
}
```

You may notice that the function returns a `Ptr<BaseOCR>`. Now, take a look at the highlighted code. It calls the create method to initialize a Tesseract OCR instance. Let's take a look at its official signature, since it allows several specific parameters:

```
Ptr<OCRTesseract> create(const char* datapath=NULL,
    const char* language=NULL,
    const char* char_whitelist=NULL,
    int oem=3, int psmode=3);
```

Let's dissect each one of these parameters:

- `datapath`: This is the path to the `tessdata` files of the root directory. The path must end with a backslash / character. The `tessdata` directory contains the language files you installed. Passing `nullptr` to this parameter will make Tesseract search in its installation directory, which is the location where this folder is normally present. It's common to change this value to `args[0]` when deploying an application and include the `tessdata` folder in your application path.

- `language`: This is a three letter word with the language code (for example, eng for English, por for Portuguese, or hin for Hindi). Tesseract supports loading of multiple language codes using the + sign. So, passing *eng+por* will load both English and Portuguese languages. Of course, you can only use languages that you previously installed; otherwise, the loading will fail. A language configuration file can specify that two or more languages must be loaded together. To prevent this, you can use a tilde ~. For example, you can use *hin+~eng* to guarantee that English is not loaded with Hindi, even if it is configured to do so.

- `whitelist`: This is the character set to be considered for recognition. If `nullptr` is passed, the characters will be 0123456789abcdefghijklmnopqrstuvwxyzABCDEFGHIJKLMNOPQRSTUVWXYZ.

- `oem`: These are OCR algorithms that will be used. They can have one of the following values:

    ○ `OEM_TESSERACT_ONLY`: This uses just Tesseract. It's the fastest method, but it also has less precision.

    ○ `OEM_CUBE_ONLY`: This uses the cube engine. It's slower, but more precise. This will only work if your language was trained to support this engine mode. To check whether that's the case, look for .cube files for your language in the `tessdata` folder. The support for English language is guaranteed.

    ○ `OEM_TESSERACT_CUBE_COMBINED`: This combines both Tesseract and cube to achieve the best possible OCR classification. This engine has the best accuracy and the slowest execution time.

    ○ `OEM_DEFAULT`: This tries to infer the strategy based in the language `config` file, command line `config` file, or in the absence of both, uses `OEM_TESSERACT_ONLY`.

- `psmode`: This is the segmentation mode. The modes are as follows:

    ○ `PSM_OSD_ONLY`: Using this mode, Tesseract will just run its preprocessing algorithms to detect orientation and script detection.

    ○ `PSM_AUTO_OSD`: This tells Tesseract to do automatic page segmentation with orientation and script detection.

    ○ `PSM_AUTO_ONLY`: This does page segmentation, but avoids doing orientation, script detection, or OCR. This is the default value.

    ○ `PSM_AUTO`: This does page segmentation and OCR, but avoids doing orientation or script detection.

    ○ `PSM_SINGLE_COLUMN`: This assumes that the text of variable sizes is displayed in a single column.

- ° PSM_SINGLE_BLOCK_VERT_TEXT: This treats the image as a single uniform block of a vertically aligned text.

- ° PSM_SINGLE_BLOCK: This is a single block of text. This is the default configuration. We will use this flag since our preprocessing phase guarantees this condition.

- ° PSM_SINGLE_LINE: This indicates that the image contains only one line of text.

- ° PSM_SINGLE_WORD: This indicates that the image contains just one word.

- ° PSM_SINGLE_WORD_CIRCLE: This informs that the image is a just one word disposed in a circle.

- ° PSM_SINGLE_CHAR: This indicates that the image contains a single character.

For the last two parameters, the #include tesseract directory recommends you to use the constant names instead of directly inserting their values.

The last step is to add text detection to our main function. To do this, just add the following code to the end of the main method:

```
auto ocr = initOCR("tesseract");
for (int i = 0; i < groups.size(); i++)
{
  Mat wordImage = drawER(channels, regions, groups[i],
    groupRects[i]);
  string word;
  ocr->run(wordImage, word);
  cout << word << endl;
}
```

In this code, we started by calling our initOCR method to create a Tesseract instance. Notice that the remaining code will not change if we choose a different OCR engine, since the run method signature is guaranteed by the BaseOCR class.

Next, we iterate over each detected ERFilter group. Since each group represents a different word, we:

- Call the previously created drawER function to create an image with the word.

- Create a text string called word, and call the run function to recognize the word image. The recognized word will be stored in the string.

- Print the text string on the screen.

Let's take a look at the run method signature. This method is defined in the `BaseOCR` class and will be equal for all specific OCR implementations, even the ones that might be implemented in the future:

```
virtual void run(Mat& image, std::string& output_text,
    std::vector<Rect>* component_rects=NULL,
    std::vector<std::string>* component_texts=NULL,
    std::vector<float>* component_confidences=NULL,
    int component_level=0) = 0;
```

Of course, this is a pure virtual function that must be implemented by each specific class (such as the `OCRTesseract` class that we just used):

- `image`: This is the input image. It must be an RGB or a grayscale image

- `component_rects`: We can provide a vector to be filled with the bounding box of each component (words or text lines) detected by the OCR engine

- `component_texts`: If given, this vector will be filled with the text strings of each component detected by the OCR

- `component_confidences`: If given, the vector will be filled with floats and the confidence values of each component

- `component_level`: This defines what a component is. It may have the `OCR_LEVEL_WORD` (by default) or `OCR_LEVEL_TEXT_LINE` values

> If necessary, we prefer changing the component level to a word or line in the `run()` method instead of doing the same thing in the `psmode` parameter of the `create()` function. This is preferable since the `run` method will be supported by any OCR engine that decides to implement the `BaseOCR` class. Always remember that the `create()` method is where vendor specific configurations are set.

This is the program's final output:

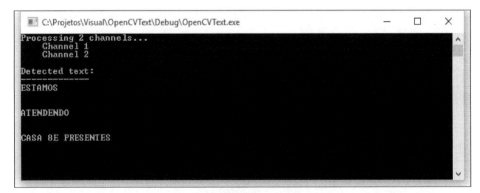

Despite a minor confusion with the & symbol, every word was perfectly recognized! You can check the complete source code in the `ocr.cpp` file, in the chapter code.

Summary

In this chapter, we saw that scene text recognition is a far more difficult OCR situation than working with scanned texts. We studied how the text module addresses this problem with extremal region identification using the **Newmann and Matas** algorithm. We also saw how to use this API with the `floodfill` function to extract the text to an image and submit it to Tesseract OCR. Finally, we studied how the OpenCV text module integrates with Tesseract and other OCR engines, and how we can use its classes to identify what's written in the image.

This ends our journey with OpenCV. From the beginning to the end of this book, we expected you to have a glance about the Computer Vision area and have a better understanding of how several applications work. We also sought to show you that, although OpenCV is quite an impressive library, the field is already full of opportunities for improvement and research.

Thank you for reading! No matter whether you use OpenCV for creating impressive commercial programs based on Computer Vision, or if you use it in a research that will change the world, we hope you will find this content useful. Just keep working with your skills—this was just the beginning!

Index

A

ANNs (artificial neural networks) 127
application
  creating, for AOI 103, 104
Automated Optical Inspection 100
automatic object inspection classification
    example 133-135

B

background subtraction
  about 164
  naive background subtraction 164-166
basic CMake configuration files 20
basic data persistence 44
basic graphical user interface
  with OpenCV 51-55
basic matrix operations 41-43
basic object types
  about 38
  Point object type 39
  Rect object type 40
  RotatedRect object type 40
  Scalar object type 39
  Size object type 40
  Vec object type 38
Black Hat transform 186
blurring 244
buttons
  adding, to user interface 63-67

C

cameras
  reading 33-37
cartoonize effect
  about 93
  creating 93-97
classifiers 253
CMake
  reference 14
CMake script file
  generating 76, 77
complex script
  creating 23-25
Computer Vision applications
  machine learning workflow 130-132
connected component algorithm 112-118
connectedComponents function
  about 114
  connectivity parameter 114
  image parameter 114
  labels parameter 114
  type parameter 115
connectedComponentsWithStats function
  about 115
  CC_STAT_AREA parameter 115
  CC_STAT_HEIGHT parameter 115
  CC_STAT_LEFT parameter 115
  CC_STAT_TO parameter 115
  CC_STAT_WIDTH parameter 115
  Centroids parameter 115
  Stats parameter 115

W

Thank you for buying
OpenCV By Example

About Packt Publishing

Packt, pronounced 'packed', published its first book, *Mastering phpMyAdmin for Effective MySQL Management*, in April 2004, and subsequently continued to specialize in publishing highly focused books on specific technologies and solutions.

Our books and publications share the experiences of your fellow IT professionals in adapting and customizing today's systems, applications, and frameworks. Our solution-based books give you the knowledge and power to customize the software and technologies you're using to get the job done. Packt books are more specific and less general than the IT books you have seen in the past. Our unique business model allows us to bring you more focused information, giving you more of what you need to know, and less of what you don't.

Packt is a modern yet unique publishing company that focuses on producing quality, cutting-edge books for communities of developers, administrators, and newbies alike. For more information, please visit our website at www.packtpub.com.

About Packt Open Source

In 2010, Packt launched two new brands, Packt Open Source and Packt Enterprise, in order to continue its focus on specialization. This book is part of the Packt Open Source brand, home to books published on software built around open source licenses, and offering information to anybody from advanced developers to budding web designers. The Open Source brand also runs Packt's Open Source Royalty Scheme, by which Packt gives a royalty to each open source project about whose software a book is sold.

Writing for Packt

We welcome all inquiries from people who are interested in authoring. Book proposals should be sent to author@packtpub.com. If your book idea is still at an early stage and you would like to discuss it first before writing a formal book proposal, then please contact us; one of our commissioning editors will get in touch with you.

We're not just looking for published authors; if you have strong technical skills but no writing experience, our experienced editors can help you develop a writing career, or simply get some additional reward for your expertise.

open source
community experience distilled

Mastering OpenCV Android
Application Programming

Mastering OpenCV Android Application Programming

ISBN: 978-1-78398-820-4   Paperback: 216 pages

Master the art of implementing computer vision algorithms on Android platforms to build robust and efficient applications

1. Understand and utilise the features of OpenCV, Android SDK, and OpenGL.

2. Detect and track specific objects in a video using Optical Flow and Lucas Kanade Tracker.

3. An advanced guide full of real-world examples, helping you to build smart OpenCV Android applications.

OpenCV Computer Vision Application
Programming Cookbook
Second Edition

OpenCV Computer Vision Application Programming Cookbook

Second Edition

ISBN: 978-1-78216-148-6   Paperback: 374 pages

Over 50 recipes to help you build computer vision applications in C++ using the OpenCV library

1. Master OpenCV, the open source library of the computer vision community.

2. Master fundamental concepts in computer vision and image processing.

3. Learn the important classes and functions of OpenCV with complete working examples applied on real images.

Please check **www.PacktPub.com** for information on our titles

Learning Image Processing with OpenCV

ISBN: 978-1-78328-765-9   Paperback: 232 pages

Exploit the amazing features of OpenCV to create powerful image processing applications through easy-to-follow examples

1. Learn how to build full-fledged image processing applications using free tools and libraries.

2. Take advantage of cutting-edge image processing functionalities included in OpenCV v3.

3. Understand and optimize various features of OpenCV with the help of easy-to-grasp examples.

OpenCV for Secret Agents

ISBN: 978-1-78328-737-6   Paperback: 302 pages

Use OpenCV in six secret projects to augment your home, car, phone, eyesight, and any photo or drawing

1. Build OpenCV apps for the desktop, the Raspberry Pi, Android, and the Unity game engine.

2. Learn real-time techniques that can be used to classify images, detecting and recognizing any person or animal, and studying motion and distance with superhuman precision.

3. Design hands-free interfaces that are practical in home automation, in cars, and in discrete surveillance.

Please check **www.PacktPub.com** for information on our titles

Made in the USA
San Bernardino, CA
04 July 2016